THE SCOTTISH TERRIER

THE 'SCOTTIE' has always been well-loved and respected by dog owners the world over.

Mrs. Caspersz, one of the foremost experts on the breed, has written a comprehensive guide which will prove of great value to both pet owner and prospective breeder alike.

THE SCOTTISH TERRIER

BY

D. S. CASPERSZ

ARCO PUBLISHING COMPANY, INC.
NEW YORK

Library of Congress Cataloging in Publication Data
Caspersz, Dorothy.
The Scottish terrier.

(Arco/Foyles pet handbooks)
Bibliography: p.
Includes index.
1. Scottish terriers. I. Title.
SF429.S4C32 636.7'55 76–11027
ISBN 0–668–03975–2

Printed in Great Britain

CONTENTS

LIST OF ILLUSTRATIONS

1

ORIGIN

THE ORIGIN of a breed of dog of such antiquity as that which is nowadays known as the Scottish Terrier, is perforce somewhat wrapped in mystery. What we do know is that several hundred years ago there existed in the Western Highlands and the Hebrides a small rough-coated terrier bred solely for work. Old pictures of the Highland terriers prior to the year 1850 prove that type was very varied. Some were depicted rather high on the leg, others low to ground; ears were sometimes erect, sometimes semi-erect; tails were invariably gaily-carried and their coats appear to have been of all sorts, from the short-haired and wiry to the shaggy, unkempt and profuse. What is probably the earliest reference to this little working terrier of Scotland, appears in a book on Natural History dated 1815. It refers to a "wiry-haired Scotch terrier bitch" owned by the governor of Surinam in 1813.

From Thomas Bell's *History of British Quadrupeds* of 1837, however, we get the first published description of the only two distinct breeds of terrier existing in Great Britain at that time. The one was described as smooth, sleek, the muzzle sharp, the body neat and compact, usually black and tan in colour; the other was called the Scotch or Wire-haired terrier, which differed from the former in the rough harsh character of the hair, the shortness and stoutness of the limbs, and in colour, which was generally a dirty white though they varied very much. Obviously we can deduce from the above that the first-named was the progenitor of the English breeds of terrier – the Black and Tan, the Manchester, and the Fox-terrier – and the second was the rough-haired little worker indigenous to Scotland.

It has long been generally accepted that the rough-coated, short-legged terrier breeds as we now know them, all came originally from the same source, that of the working terrier of the Scottish Highlands. These include the Scottish Terrier (as now known), the Cairn, the West Highland White, and most probably also the Yorkshire Terrier. Some think that the Skye Terrier and also the Dandie Dinmont likewise come from the Scottish original, though it is believed these two breeds had for a longer period been bred true to a type. That one or both of them however, were ultimately used as a cross with the smaller longer-legged type of Scotch terrier, to produce the heavier-boned Aberdeen, as our breed was once called, is not beyond the bounds of probability. In the very earliest days of the Scottie as a show breed, such features as coat-texture, colour, and extreme length of back, were suggestive of such crosses.

It must be remembered that the Highlands in those far-off days were very wild and not easily accessible to travellers. Consequently, the strains or packs of terriers kept for work may have varied considerably in type, according to the requirements in the different localities, and also to any personal preferences of their owners. Pluck and stamina would be the main factors in selection, regardless of pedigree, and any intermingling with blood from other strains would be unlikely. It has been recorded that the Macdonalds of Skye had a preference for the long-coated and long-bodied type; and that the Malcolms of Poltalloch selected for the pale coloured and short-coated terrier; thus were the Skye Terrier and the West Highland White, as we now know them, evolved.

The first dog show ever held in Britain took place in 1859, but it was not until twenty years later that classes were put on at the Kennel Club show for what were variously described as "Scotch, Hard-haired, or Broken-haired Terriers". At about the same time, the first Standard of Points ever arrived at for our breed was drawn up. This gives a detailed description of every feature, and lays particular stress on the dog being thick-set, strong and compact, with a coat that should be both fairly short and very hard. The average size, indicated by weight, is given as sixteen lb. to seventeen lb. for dogs, and two lb. less for bitches. The approved colours were "various shades of grey, or grizzle" and brindle, the most desirable colour being red brindle, with black muzzle and "ear-tips".

That there is never any mention of all-black dogs in those early days is worth noting. Black as a colour for a Scottie was never known until about 1890, and it was not until 1930 that it was in any sense popularized.

The region of Scotland from which the show type of Scottish Terrier was mainly evolved was the Blackmount part of Perthshire, the Moor of Rannoch, and surrounding districts. About the year 1880 a certain Captain Mackie made a driving tour through this area, in search of terriers. This is recounted in Mr. Thomson Gray's monograph on the breed, published in 1887. Captain Mackie visited fox-hunters who had owned the same strain of terriers for sixty years and more, and the dogs he bought on this tour were among those which went to found the existing breed of Scottish Terriers.

It is impossible to say now, after nearly eighty years of being bred to a standard and for exhibition, which of the present-day Scottish breeds of short-legged terrier most resembles the common progenitor they undoubtedly shared. The earliest of the show Scots, when they were popularly known as Aberdeens, certainly bore more resemblance to the modern Cairn than anything else.

The breed, above all else, was originally a working breed, and it behoves modern breeders to select for hardihood and gameness along with external points, never losing sight of the original purpose for which the breed existed, otherwise the essential characteristics may be lost. Every breed of dog had an original purpose, and though the show-ring is our only guide as to external virtues, it provides no tests for the innate terrier instincts of going to ground and for killing vermin. The Scottie is a tough little customer, of immense independence and indomitable courage, with a large head and immensely big teeth for his size, and a body indicative of great strength and substance in small compass. He is able and willing, if need arises, to do battle with adversaries more than twice his own size, and can fight to the death, which quality earned him the fitting title of "Diehard". Prospective owners of a specimen of the breed would therefore do well to insist that his general appearance and behaviour indicate his suitability for the work for which he was originally kept in his native environment. He may seldom have a chance to do it, but the instincts are there and should be preserved.

2

HISTORY

It was around the year 1880 that the Scottish Terrier, from being something of Scotland's very own, came to be seen, known and appreciated in England. To Mr. H. J. Ludlow, founder of the first Scottish Terrier Club (the S.T.C.Eng.) in 1883, belongs most of the credit for popularizing the breed in the south. He bred or owned many of the earliest Champions. By that time classes for the breed were being scheduled at all the more important shows. It is worthy of note that among the prizewinners of those days were several dogs amd bitches whose direct descendants are winning today. What is even more remarkable is that every known representative of our breed traces back in direct male line to a dog named Bonaccord, a winner of the period 1879-80. Thus, basically there is only one male line of descent throughout the entire breed, though of course innumerable branches and ramifications have been developed from it since. Bonaccord had a son named Rambler, a dog which was evidently used extensively at stud. Rambler sired several Champions, among them being the two dogs Ch. Dundee and Ch. Alister. Dundee was the result of mating Rambler to his half-sister; Alister was by Rambler out of one of his Champion grand-daughters. These two half-brothers, Dundee and Alister, who may truly be described as the pillars of the breed, were said to differ somewhat in type and to beget puppies showing this same divergence. Dundee was a brindle dog, weighing twenty-four lb., reputed to have been very heavily built and possessing overlarge ears. Alister was apparently a more refined type, and, strangely enough – since black as a colour in those early days was almost unknown – was a black dog.

In-breeding was much resorted to in those days. Whether it was due to shortage of material or because the pioneer breeders were determined to fix what by then had come to be the accepted type, we can only guess. Whatever the reason, certain it is that a definite breed type was established for all time, and though, during the ensuing seventy or more years, the influence of the show-ring has modified it and effected improvements in detail, the fundamental requirements remain practically unaltered. Evidence of this is provided by reference to the first breed standard drawn up in 1879, where certain basic features are described which are desired every bit as much today as they were then. Take for instance these excerpts quoted from the old standard. "A muscular form, fitting him for the most arduous work; and sagacity, intelligence and courage to make the most of the situation . . .". "The head is longish." "The muzzle very powerful; there must be no approach to snipishness." "The eyes are small, well sunk in the head, dark hazel, bright and expressive, with heavy eyebrows." "Ears very small and free from long hair, feather, or fringe." "The neck is short, thick and very muscular, well set between the shoulders and showing great power." "The body gives an impression of great strength . . . the chest is broad and deep . . . the back broad; the loins broad and very strong . . . the body is covered with a dense, hard and wet-resisting coat of about two inches long." "The forelegs are straight, with immense bone for a dog of this size; elbows in same plane as shoulder-joints and not outside, the forearm being particularly muscular; the hind legs are also strong, the thighs being well developed and thick, the hocks well bent . . ."

It will be seen that the main characteristics are still unchanged today; great strength and muscular power has always been stressed. True, Dame Fashion has played some unfortunate tricks with reference to Necks and Coats, for no longer is the neck expected to be "short", though it is still required to be "very muscular"; and since the date when the Kennel Club permitted trimming with knives, scissors and so forth, coats immediately deteriorated, becoming far too profuse, lengthy and often wavy.

For about the first twenty years of show-ring influence on the breed, the exhibits sometimes presented a very mixed assortment indeed. Modern admirers of the Scot would find it difficult to conjure up in their imaginations a picture of a judging-ring of those times. Right on until 1910 types were very varied. There were bat ears, yellow eyes, curly tails, bowed fronts, overlong bodies, and some terrible hindquarters, as well as sometimes a silky coat suggestive of a Skye or Yorkshire cross. "Hope springs eternal", and no doubt the exhibitors of the times were optimists. Judging, in consequence, was far more difficult than it is nowadays.

In 1883 the Scottish Terrier Club (England) was founded, followed in 1888 by the Scottish Terrier Club (Scotland). Both these societies adopted a Standard of Points which agreed in almost every particular, and by 1909 a few outstanding terriers conforming more closely to this standard had made their appearance. The majority of the best were still kennelled in Scotland, the well-known prefixes of "Claymore", "Merlewood" and "Ornsay" holding sway. But in England, the "Ems", "Laindon", "Bapton", and ultimately "Albourne" kennels were rapidly making their presence felt, and by 1915 honours were about even both sides of the Border.

By that time, black had become both prevalent and popular as a colour, and around 1927 to 1935 it was unusual to find any other colours among the prizewinners. Now, these twenty years later, an all-black among any representative entry at a show is the exception rather than the rule. The inevitable swing of the pendulum has resuscitated the various workaday colours which were characteristic of the breed in its early days. Unfortunately, a large proportion of the unenlightened general public still suffer from the delusion that the Scot ought to be black, but they are learning, albeit slowly, that it is becoming increasingly hard to buy one of that colour, and that the endless choice of reds, greys, browns, wheatens and brindles provide precisely the same unique temperament with the added charm of variety.

As one looks back at photographs of the more notable dogs prior to around 1937, a marked contrast is discernible as regards coat, as compared to the dog of modern times. Until then, the good specimen appeared to be higher on the leg than he actually was, owing to the businesslike shortness of his coat, which was seldom more than one-and-a-half to two inches in length on any part of him. Profusion of coat followed on the heels of the black craze. Previously, such things as exaggerated feathering, fantastic beards, and long soft-textured hair under the body, were unheard of. For a period after the second World War, these superfluous embellishments were cultivated to excess and utilized to deceive the judges while covering a multitude of faults. However, as the judges got wise to it, a reasonable modification came about. Though the coats of the modern dog are inevitably too long if left in a state of nature, it is now taken for granted that the Scottish Terrier is a breed that looks the better for being trimmed, and trimming has reached a fine art which is carried out in most cases with skill and moderation. The coat of good hard texture does not need such drastic trimming as the bad soft coat, so, luckily for the breed there is still the incentive to breed them with the "dense, hard, wet-resisting" jacket.

The surest guide as to the popularity of any breed of dog is offered by the registration totals published each month by the Kennel Club. From these one realizes how some breeds have a sudden rise to fame, and for a few years their registration totals reach fantastic heights. Then just as suddenly they appear to lose favour and the figures drop month by month. In the case of the Scottie, it may be said his general popularity, as indicated by K.C. registrations, has been maintained steadily on a fairly even keel throughout the years ever since pedigrees were first recorded. True, for a short time he figured quite near the top of the list of breeds, contesting in popular favour with the Cocker spaniels and the Pekinese, but his present position is usually about thirteenth or fourteenth in order of registration totals of all breeds, and, as there are about 110 breeds accounted for, it is obvious that Scottish Terriers rank among the better liked and more widely owned of all breeds of dog.

I. BONNYTON TOFF. Black brindle dog, well known winner about 1913.

II. CHAMPION TIP O'DEESIDE. Black dog, bred by Dr. J. B. Pitt, 1916.

III. ALBOURNE ANNIE LAURIE. Red brindle bitch, bred by Miss I. Wijk about 1924. Famous as the dam of six Champions.

IV. GARRELL TODDLER. Black dog bred by Mr. W. Erskine. 1928. Sire of a Champion and many winners.

V. CHAMPION HEATHER REALISATION. Grey brindle dog bred by Mr. Robt. Chapman, born 1934. Holds the record for the greatest number of Challenge Certificates (47) ever won by one of the breed.

VI. CHAMPION DESCO DESIRE. Black bitch bred by Mrs. L. J. Dewar, 1935.

VII. TURFIELD MY LAD. Black dog bred by Mrs. D. S. Caspersz, 1942.

3

DESCRIPTION AND STANDARD OF THE BREED

THE SCOTTISH TERRIER is a very sturdily built short-legged dog, with a harsh, double, weather-resisting coat which may be any colour in the world except white, small prick ears and a neat shortish tail carried gaily upwards. His height at shoulder is about ten inches, his weight around twenty-one lb. The general impression he should give is one of great strength and solidity in small compass, yet possessed of surprising agility; the head carried with dignity, the face wearing an expression of bright enquiry and alert intelligence. He should move with an air of firmness and independence.

The Standard of the Breed, as revised by the Scottish Terrier Club (Eng.) in 1932, was later adopted and authorized by the Kennel Club, and is as follows:

GENERAL APPEARANCE. A Scottish Terrier is a sturdy, thick-set dog of a size to get to ground, placed on short legs, alert in carriage, and suggestive of great power and activity in small compass. The head gives the impression of being long for a dog of its size. The body is covered with a close-lying, broken, rough-textured coat, and with keen intelligent eyes and sharp prick ears, the dog looks willing to go anywhere and do anything. In spite of its short legs, the construction of the dog enables it to be very agile and active. The whole movement of the dog is smooth, easy and straightforward, with free action at shoulder, stifle and hock.

HEAD AND SKULL. Without being out of proportion to the size of the dog it should be long, the length of skull enabling it to be fairly wide and yet retain a narrow appearance. The skull is nearly flat and the cheekbones do not protrude. There is a slight, but distinct drop between skull and foreface just in front of the eye. The nose is large, and in profile, the line from the nose towards the chin appears to slope backwards.

EYES. Should be almond-shaped, dark brown, fairly wide apart and set deeply under the eyebrows.

EARS. Neat, of fine texture, pointed and erect.

MOUTH. Teeth large, the upper incisors closely overlapping the lower.

NECK. Muscular, of moderate length.

FOREQUARTERS. The head is carried on a muscular neck of moderate length showing quality, set into a long sloping shoulder, the brisket well in front of the forelegs, which are straight, well-boned to straight pasterns. The chest is fairly broad and hung between the forelegs, which must not be out at elbows nor placed under the body.

BODY. The body has well-rounded ribs, which flatten to a deep chest and are carried well back. The back is proportionately short and very muscular. In general, the top line of the body should be straight; the loin muscular and deep, thus powerfully coupling the ribs to the hindquarters.

HINDQUARTERS. Remarkably powerful for the size of the dog. Big and wide buttocks. Thighs deep and muscular, well bent at stifle. Hocks strong and well bent and neither turned inwards nor outwards.

FEET. Of good size and well padded, toes well arched and close-knit.

TAIL. Of moderate length to give a a general balance to the dog, thick at the root and tapering towards the tip, is set on with an upright carriage or with a slight bend.

COAT. The dog has two coats, the undercoat short, dense and soft; the outercoat harsh, dense, and wiry; the two making a weather-resisting covering to the dog.

COLOUR. Black, wheaten, or brindle of any colour.

WEIGHT AND SIZE. The ideally made dog in hard show condition could weigh from nineteen lb. to twenty-three lb. Height at shoulder ten to eleven inches.

There are certain phrases in this standard to which the very greatest importance should be attached, because they allude to features which provide the keynote to the right type. "Of a size to get to ground" is clear indication that the breed must not be allowed to get too big. The standard weight was recently altered from seventeen to twenty-one lb. to nineteen to twenty-three lb. simply because, although the dog remained the same size so far as measurements were concerned, he was being bred with heavier bone and greater substance throughout, consequently the top winners were found to be always nearer twenty-three than twenty-one lb. Size and weight are ever deceptive, but this very wise clause at the beginning of the Standard is intended to safeguard us from the monsters turning the scales at twenty-six lb. and over, which have at times been seen in the show-ring. It has always been easier to breed an outstandingly good specimen whose only fault is oversize, than one as good of the right size. The American market, however, is for those well within the standard weight, and the ordinary buying public invariably prefer the small one of handy size.

The "eyes almond-shaped" and "fairly wide apart" is another typical characteristic, and even more so is the drop or "stop" between skull and foreface, and the slightly receding profile from nose to chin. These are distinguishing characteristics of a good head, which differentiate the Scot entirely from other terrier breeds.

In the paragraph on Forequarters, emphasis should be placed on the brisket being "well in front of the forelegs". It is an old saying that when viewing the dog in profile there should be as much of a Scot in front of his forelegs as there is behind them. Though a slight exaggeration this is usefully descriptive and conveys the right idea. In the same paragraph we read that the "chest is fairly broad and hung between the forelegs". Again this is a peculiarity of great importance, ensuring as it should that the dog is low-swung and not having the body placed, as it were, on top of the legs. One of the worst faults in a Scot is to be narrow-fronted.

Possibly the clearest indication of correct breed type is

supplied by hindquarters of the right formation. Together with big ribs, which are "carried well back", the exceptionally powerful hindquarters, with their breadth of thigh and well-bent stifle (knee-joint), are most typical and very essential characteristics. Such hindquarters provide the springing ability which is often quite surprising; a well-constructed dog from a standing start can often jump on to a bench or table three times his own height.

The typical gait of a Scot is of considerable importance, and should indicate his correct build. It implies freedom of movement at shoulder, elbow, stifle and hock joints. He is a small dog, but built on big lines, and though low to ground his unique conformation enables him to be particularly active and agile. When moving at the trot his legs should travel in a straight fore and aft direction, with no tendency to any side-swing, and he should take very long strides.

4

CHARACTER

JUST AS his contours and outward appearance are unique among dogs, so also is the character of the Scottish Terrier. In him we have a friend and companion second to none. He has so many attributes which appeal. He is of a handy size and a serviceable colour, with the sort of coat-texture that, after a shake or two and a chance to rub himself dry, does not harbour wet or mud to any extent. He is also hardy, and possessed of amazing adaptability. He is a true Scot, in the sense that he is of a reserved nature, not addicted to gushing or unnecessary chatter. His affection is not given to all and sundry; he is discriminating and a wonderful judge of human beings. It is impossible for there to be a Scottie as a member of a household without everyone being aware of the fact, for he concerns himself with and keeps a watchful eye on everything that happens, and abounds in sympathetic understanding of all human vagaries. Usually he prefers to single out one person for his devotion, but evinces a well-bred tolerance of other people. Essentially gentlemanly, he has an innate dignity all his own, and is not, as a rule, given to scrapping. If battles have to be fought, he can hold his own as a true Diehard, when his tough skin and protective double coat save him many an injury, but he does not look for trouble. He is much more concerned with sharing his owner's interests, and any opportunities, should they occur, of showing his prowess as a destroyer of vermin. He has a very keen nose for such things, and is a first-class burrower. With his powerful teeth and strong paws he can dig a large hole nearly as quickly as any man with a spade! And how he enjoys the job!

Independence is one of his strongest qualities. Some think him obstinate, but these do not rightly understand the Scottish temperament. He is exceedingly wise, he thinks and works things out for himself, and naturally has a mind of his own. He may tax your patience at times, for if, in his opinion, your demands are trifling or unreasonable, he can put on a deliberately stubborn act and obey only at his own speed. In such cases the dog is usually right if we have the humility to admit it, and he will do less than nothing for you if you shout at or punish him harshly. His hearing is much more acute than your own, and if you have won and deserve his affection, and treat him with respect and firm gentleness, he is quickly responsive. He really has an inborn desire to please, and there are no limits to his ability to learn whatever he may be taught to do, provided he is given praise and appreciation when it is earned. For he is immensely sensitive to praise or blame. Philosophical in demeanour, it is not in his scheme of things to show his feelings too much, but that he has very deep feelings is frequently demonstrated by the contrasting behaviour of the dog in an atmosphere of love and appreciation, or the same dog encountering continual disapproval and anger. Just the difference between a happy dog and one that is misunderstood, and a misunderstood Scottie is indeed a pitiable sight.

There is much truth in the saying that one does not own a Scottie; one is owned by him. For he is somewhat possessive in his devotion, and can suffer jealousy, though he has a dour and retiring way of displaying this emotion. He is a sharp guard, giving alarm only when necessary, and will defend his own house and garden, ever on the alert to tackle unwanted intruders like cats or virmin. One of his most pleasing qualities is the restrained use he makes of his bark. If properly brought up he is not given to barking unnecessarily. One would assume he is a believer in the old adage "actions speak lounder than words". He expresses his thoughts, wishes, and intentions most clearly by means of his ears, his eyes and his tail. One can hold an intelligent conversation with such a dog; though you may do all the talking, his eyes and ears will register more understanding and response than most people's faces. And the more you treat him like the wise and reasoning personality that he is, the more will you enjoy his company, the more you will learn from him, and the cleverer will he become. As one's Scot pal grows old, he grows uncannily wise. Somebody once said "if they lived as long as we do they'd be too clever to live with".

The Scot is seemingly aloof, highly independent, sensitive, hates above all things to be stared at or watched, but is invariably a great character. One of his many charms is his sense of humour. His playfulness and love of fun are often maintained right on into old age. But never laugh at him; laugh with him. In fact, to get the best from him all his life, treat him with respect, for though small in stature he is great in heart and, when properly understood, big in mind. Of all the terrier tribe he is the safest playmate for children, being tolerant, adaptable and slow to anger.

5

HOW TO SELECT A PUPPY

THE CHOICE of a puppy must depend somewhat upon whether you require it mainly as a pet and house-dog, or for ultimate showing and breeding. Certain principles apply to both, such as health, condition and temperament, but you do not need to be so fussy over the pedigree of your pet. In fact some breeders sell some of their pal-type pups without pedigree, when such pups carry a definite blemish, in the hope that it will not become known from what stock the faulty one descended.

There are several ways of discovering where to apply for a typical, healthy well-reared puppy. Be sure to buy from the kennels of a reputable breeder. Perusal of the advertisement columns in the weekly canine papers may give a good idea where some of these are to be found, but if in any doubt, ring up or write to the Kennel Club (1-4 Clarges Street, Piccadilly) for guidance and you will be given names and addresses of dependable breeders. Make up your mind as to about what price you are prepared to pay, and state this amount when enquiring from a breeder. It is better to know at the outset if the sort of puppy you visualized cannot be bought at the figure you had in mind, than to risk rubbing up the serious breeder entirely the wrong way by saying that you "only want a throw-out as a pet" or that you "don't mind if it is not pure-bred", or, worse than all, describe in detail all the points you expect your puppy to possess (virtually a potential winner) and say you will give a fiver for it. Breeders do not spend their time, money and thought producing throw-outs or mongrels, nor do they breed primarily for the pet buyer. It is incidental to dog-breeding that one cannot keep all the pups one breeds, and the pet market is supplied from surplus stock, stock that is typical, well-reared and of the highest lineage but just misses showing sufficient promise to make a top-flighter for exhibition. Moreover, puppies cost something to rear, and since most commodities have risen to three or four times their pre-war value, the price of a decently reared puppy which at eight weeks old would have been five guineas before the last war, is nowadays anything from twelve to twenty guineas.

You may be prepared to house-train a young puppy and take it at eight or ten weeks old, or the youngster of around six months which is already trained to lead may have a stronger appeal. The latter costs considerably more than the former, which is only natural, since, if a breeder has kept one on to that age it is usually because he considers it worth showing or breeding from, consequently there are not many in the market of around six months except at a price commensurate with their potential value.

If possible, visit the kennel, from which you think of buying a pet-puppy, or get a nearby friend on whose description you can rely, to do so. Disabuse your mind at the start of any preference and prejudice as regards coat-colour. In the four-legged companion that is going to share your life for maybe twelve or fourteen years if you care for him properly, it is character and brains you want, and these qualities are inherent in the Scot, be he grey, brown, wheaten, black, or a mingling of all the prevailing coat-colours. Stipulating one particular colour in the puppy you seek limits your choice unnecessarily. The breed has always offered a wide range of colours, and a glance into a modern show-ring proves that the variety of shades is greater now than ever, but it is merely a foolish notion to imagine that coat colour has any bearing whatever on intelligence. Moreover, should you decide one day that your pet has matured into such a good-looker that you try your hand as an exhibitor, his colour will be entirely immaterial, for "a good dog, like a good horse, cannot be a bad colour".

In selecting a pal from among a bunch of pups, look for the one that carries itself with an air of independence, one that evinces curiosity, looks questioningly at you, and has a gaily-carried tail. Avoid the sluggish-looking, or one that runs away and hides at the sight or sound of your approach. Never pick up a puppy of someone else's until you have asked for, or been given permission to do so. When allowed to examine it on a table, look for the signs of good health – a loose body skin which, when grasped by the hand, crinkles up easily into folds; a bright clear eye; ears which are clean inside; gums of a healthy pink; the coat smelling sweet and clean, and free of lice, nits or such-like; a tail which feels thick at the root. Examine the underside of the puppy, making sure there are no spots or suggestions of redness in the armpits or under the thighs. At eight weeks old a healthy puppy should feel fat but firm-fleshed. At three or four months it should still be well covered with flesh but feel harder and more muscular, with sturdy legs and thickly padded feet. If there is any choice in coat textures, you will be wise if you do not fall for the fuzzy bewhiskered pup, quaint though he may look, but rather choose the smoother close-coated one which may appear somewhat plain beside his fellows, and has no sign of what are called furnishings. These will develop later, and he will be a hard-coated dog, and in consequence very much easier to keep clean and tidy all his life.

When buying a puppy for either show or breeding, or both, there is very much more to be considered. The foregoing recommendations concerning health, cleanliness and temperament of course apply equally, but now pedigree and points are additional factors of the greatest importance. It is more than ever necessary to deal with a kennel of repute. Try and see the parents of any puppy you are considering, more especially the dam, and observe whether she is sound and healthy and in which features she excels or fails. Study the pedigree, and do not be unduly impressed by the number of names in it carrying the magic title "Ch.". Only a favoured few among the breed's champions have the capacity to sire stock anywhere near as good as themselves. What matters far more is that the bitch blood in the pedigree (the bottom line of names on an ordinary pedigree form) should belong to one of the recorded Families,*

* Scottish Terriers are among the very few breeds of dog for which full records have been compiled on what is known as the Bruce Lowe Figure System. This system sets out every Line and Family that has ever been productive of British Champions, traced down from the breed's

and that the whole pedigree of three generations or more shows some link-up in blood – in other words a certain amount of line-breeding to individuals which were good in themselves. This subject is alluded to again in the chapter on Breeding.

If you are a newcomer to the breed, and look forward to doing some showing and breeding in due course, do not make the common mistake of buying both a dog and a bitch puppy. Concentrate on a bitch. She will, if she turns out well, fulfil all functions. According to the age at which you buy it, the points to look for when picking a good one vary somewhat. If one of six to ten months of age can be afforded, so much the better, for by that age you can be more certain of what you are getting. Buying an eight to ten-week-old pup is always a bit of a gamble, unless you are an experienced puppy-picker. Even then, you have to take a chance on colour of eye and how the permanent teeth may come through, for these are matters which cannot be finally assessed until the pup is anyway past five-and-a-half months old. However, if you place your trust in the breeder of repute, quite often they can give sound advice and a fairly accurate prophecy on the ultimate merits or defects of a very young pup, because they know the tendencies and potentialities of the material from which they have bred it.

Short, straight, well-boned forelegs, moderate breadth of chest, deep brisket, ribs that are broad where they leave the spine, also deep and carried well back, strong loin, big powerful quarters, and a thick root to the tail, are all features to look for in a good puppy of any age, but at eight weeks do not expect an adult pattern of head. In fact this would be undesirable. It is often said that the puppy which looks like a mature dog in

origin. The word Line, in this connection, means solely the male line– the sire, the sire's sire, and so on, right back to the first known male parent. The word Family means only the direct female line–the dam, the dam's dam, and so on, back to the first known founder bitch of each family. These records were first published in 1934, in the work *Scottish Terrier Pedigrees*, and the figure system of classification has been universally adopted for reference, by breeders throughout the world. The reference, therefore, to a recorded Family, means one which has at some time in its history produced one or more Champions.

miniature at eight weeks, and probably has its ears erect very early, ends up by being short in head and light of bone, and there is much truth in this.

The biggest thing about an eight-week puppy should appear to be its head. The size is mainly in the skull, which should be long, high and fairly broad. This well-domed skull at the age flattens out later and develops into the desired long clean head The foreface should be broad too and very deep, but not especially long. Don't be misled by the attractions of a lean, narrow skull at this age; even though it may be high in the dome, it will not be a long head at the finish. To get an impression of how the ears are placed in relation to the skull, and whether they will be small pointed ears not too wide at the lobes, lay the puppy over on its back on the floor so that its ears fall into their erect position. One cannot hope to tell very much regarding the action of an eight-week pup, but while they are cruising around free, make sure the one you fancy travels firmly and squarely on all fours, has no tendency to cow-hocks when viewed from the rear, and does not hunch the back, or plait the front legs, or proceed all the time at a gallop when the speed would indicate a trot.

Having approved of the pedigree and seen one or both of the parents if possible, look for a gay, confident, and fairly friendly temperament in the six-month-old bitch you may contemplate buying. She need not be gushing, for a slight hesitancy or reserve with complete strangers is typically Scottish and natural, but she must on no account be shy. Then see her moving. Nothing more clearly demonstrates correct breed type than movement showing free action at shoulder, stifle and hock. If she is properly constructed she will have a long free stride, her head will be carried proudly on a strong, graceful neck of moderate length, the top line of her back will appear level, and the tail gaily carried, which means it continues from the spine in a gentle upward curve, and tapers towards the tip. Avoid the sort of tail that either leaves the back at too sharp an angle, or is definitely a curled tail, or one that can be carried laid right along the back, squirrel fashion. These, besides being faulty, are very unsightly and always conspicuous, and once introduced into your stock are mighty hard to eradicate. There is much character displayed by the proportionate and well-carried tail of a Scot, so it deserves almost as much care in selection as does the head. Having seen the bitch move freely and well and been attracted by her general appearance, have her on a table and go carefully over each point.

Her head should look long for her size and age. It should be clean-skulled, which means no bumps along the top surface of the skull, and no bulge of either bone or fat on the cheeks. There should be good strength and depth of foreface, "well filled up", as it is called, before the eyes, which means the opposite of being sunken. There must be the characteristic stop, or drop, between the eyes; viewed in profile, the top line of the foreface is just the depth of the stop below the top line of the skull. Do not look for too narrow a head. The skull should appear long from ears to eyes, and the foreface must be almost as long, but a certain width of skull proportionate to the substantially built body is in accordance with the Standard. Besides aiding the true expression it ensures enough width between the eyes, for the eyes should be set fairly wide apart. Examine the teeth, which should be large for a dog of the size, white, even and very strong, the mouth closing with a scissor-like grip, i.e. the upper incisors fitting closely over the lower. Make sure the four canine teeth, or tusks, are fully developed and that they interlock when the mouth is closed.

Eye and expression are most important. The expression can never be right unless the eyes are correctly shaped and placed. The eye itself is best described by the term almond-shaped. Its outer corner should appear to be a little higher than the inner corner; at its broadest part it is somewhat oblique; a round or full eye is a serious failing. They should be small, but not so small as to be pig-like, and must be deeply set well under the brows. The colour should always be a very dark brown, and it must be remembered that the ultimate colour is not finally established until quite five-and-a-half months of age, sometimes later.

The ears should be neat, pointed, and fine in texture. Most modern Scots have their ears erect by six or seven months, but occasionally a bitch may be a little late, even ten or eleven months, the ears only becoming firmly erect after her first season.

Never buy a young bitch which fails in hindquarters, or whose dam is not strong in that feature. Good hindquarters are necessary in the show ring, but they are essential from a breeding standpoint.

When all is said and done, and you have the choice of a few of different ages and different prices, other things being equal, pick the one whose personality appeals to you and with which you feel instinctively in sympathy; such a bitch will do better for you and be happier than one which may have the looks but a disposition out of harmony with your own.

A few final tips on selection: avoid at all costs the narrow-chested, the shallow-ribbed, the thin-footed and the slim-hipped specimens. As regards coat, follow the hint given to the buyers of a companion, for a hard coat pays dividends in any capacity and is strongly hereditary.

6

GENERAL MANAGEMENT

No ONE SHOULD should buy a puppy, or indeed keep a dog at all, unless they are prepared to look after it properly. Before undertaking the responsibility and enjoying the privilege of owning a Scottie, therefore, it is as well to give the matter some thought and consider whether its housing, feeding, training, exercise, and cleanliness will all receive proper attention. It is best if only one member of a household takes on the care of the dog, someone blessed with commonsense, a real love of dogs, and sufficient time at their disposal. Happy is the dog that can rely at all times on an understanding owner. The ideal partnership between owner and dog is one built up on mutual respect and affection; where the owner can view with pride the health, happiness and good behaviour of the dog, and the dog in return gives that sympathetic response and undying devotion which is beyond price.

HOUSING. Whether the dog is to live in the house or to occupy a building separate from the human habitation, it is essential he should have a sleeping-place he can look upon as his own. If indoors, whatever sort of bed is provided should be raised at least a couple of inches from the floor. Even the best of houses always have a floor-draught, which is the reason dogs seek the comfort of an armchair unless their own beds are similarly raised from floor level. Whatever form of bed you give, besides having it raised – two inches for a small puppy, but quite six inches for an adult – be sure it has a back and two sides of adequate height to keep away a lot of draught. Dogs cannot sleep contentedly in a draught. The form of bed Scots like best is a covered wooden box open only at one side or end. They appreciate the "ceiling" to their bed, since cold air can blow down on them from an open window. The size of the box need not be more than twenty inches square for an adult dog, and only fifteen inches in height. The cosier the better. Several layers of newspaper make a good warm lining for the bottom of it, on which place either a removable stuffed pad or fitting mattress, covered with sacking or some untearable material, or else a piece of blanket.

If the dog is to sleep in an outside unheated building, the covered box bed is an absolute essential. As he grows older and can jump higher, raise the bed still more from floor level; twelve inches is none too much. Have a low ledge fixed across the front edge of such box to keep the bedding in place. It is important that any outside accommodation for the dog should be stoutly constructed and be absolutely weather-proof. If built of wood, the walls should be double. It should be light and well ventilated, the windows opening above the dog's reach, and its door should be well-fitting and wide enough to permit the owner to get inside to reach and clean the whole place easily. The floor space allotted to one dog, or a bitch with puppies, should not be less than six feet by four feet: more if possible. The best flooring is wood, but if it happens to be concrete or brick place large removable boards over the greater part of it so that the dog has no chance of lying about on a cold surface. Provided such a dwelling is absolutely free from draughts and damp, and the dog is not subjected to sudden changes of temperature, such as being cosseted indoors one moment and banished to his kennel the next, Scots are hardy and can stand a good deal of cold, given a well-raised bed. It is damp and draughts, and having no place but a floor to sleep on, that kill. In severe weather be extra generous with more bedding or blankets in the sleeping box.

FEEDING. Under this heading comes the first and foremost necessity of every dog's internal economy; that is fresh, clean cold drinking-water, easily accessible to him at all times and frequently replenished.

For hints on the feeding of a young puppy, consult Chapter 8. Adult dogs require only one main meal per day. The best and most natural time to give it is in the evening, for a dog sleeps more soundly and contentedly through the night after a good supper. Use, as the basic essentials, good fresh lean meat;

fairly stale wholemeal bread converted into rusks in a slow oven; raw eggs; and an occasional big raw beef bone. The meat can be either beef or mutton, with only occasional changes to such items as sheep's paunch, cow's udder, or the various kinds of offal. If horse-flesh has to be resorted to, give less of it in quantity that one would use of beef, for it is apt to be scouring in effect. Have also a supply of the best quality biscuit meal, terrier grade, of which a dry handful can be mixed with the meat for the dog's supper. In these days one can buy a pure wholemeal biscuit food (such as "Laughing Dog" brand) direct from the makers. Unless your meat supply comes fresh from the butcher's it is advisable to partly cook it all, either by baking or boiling, and, by way of a change on some nights, the resulting broth from boiled meat can be poured over some biscuit meal. If this is done, however, get it only to a crumbly and nearly dry consistency before using. Never give sloppy wet food, unless it be egg and milk. About once a week, add a raw egg to the supper mixture. Eggs are particularly helpful for conditioning, and especially good for the stud dog or the breeding bitch. Also, about once a week, a feed of well-boiled herrings is useful. Boil them till they practically fall away from the bones, and all that is necessary then is to remove heads, backbones and tails. Mash up the remainder with a little dry fine-grade biscuit-meal, or with wholemeal rusk-crumbs. Dogs love it, but it is a fattening dish so do not overdo it.

In the morning the dog looks for and enjoys either a dry rusk (about the size of half a slice off a large loaf) or a hard biscuit to break his fast. If using any form of dog biscuit, avoid the small ones no larger than an inch square. These are too small for the dog to consider they have to be chewed, consequently he is apt to either swallow them whole or get one jammed across the roof of his mouth, both very undesirable happenings. Remember the dog's big moment of the day is his carefully prepared supper, which in winter should be given with the chill taken off. Keep in mind that dry food is better every time than wet. Dry feeding aids digestion and promotes a healthy thirst, therefore keep that water-bowl clean, sweet and always full. Always feed the dog in the same place and at the same hours each day. Never leave his empty dish around, and if he perchance leaves a portion of his food, take it away at once and make his supper the next night somewhat smaller. Regularity of feeding and sensible rationing of amounts is important. The Scot is by nature a greedy feeder, and to be kept fit must not be allowed all he thinks he could consume, so it is up to his owner to exercise discretion in this direction on his behalf, knowing it is far better to be slightly hungry and fit than to be overfed and sick. An item not absolutely necessary but one which keeps your dog happy is a wee "night-cap" of a tablespoonful of warm milk on retiring for the night; especially is it appreciated in winter time.

TRAINING. A completely undisciplined dog is nothing but a nuisance to its owner and a menace to everyone else. Training in its simplest form can begin while still in the nest. Scotties are exceedingly sensitive to praise or blame. They will not let this be seen immediately from their behaviour, because they hate to show their feelings, but you can be quite sure that whichever is meted out will be stored up in their experience and revealed in subsequent reactions. They are also creatures of habit and routine, and association of ideas is very strong in them. If a puppy is acquired at eight weeks old, it takes but a few days for it to interpret every varying shade of tone in its owner's voice. Which is one reason for the desirability of only one person having the sole care of the dog, its feeding, training and all else. A puppy being shouted at by one person, pushed around by another, encouraged and blamed alternately by all and sundry, stands but a poor chance of growing into a pleasant, well-mannered dog. His mental well-being is every bit as important as his physical, and it is up to the owner to be consistently kind, firm and understanding right from the start. Remember the character of the dog is formed in the early months of his life, and above all things be consistent. Habits, both good and bad, are easily formed, but not so easily cured Little tricks of behaviour, such as jumping up at you, or giving tongue every time a bell rings, may be thought highly amusing in a pup, but unless discouraged at the outset they become incurable habits, and the muddy paws and the raucous voice of the adult dog cease to be at all funny. So begin as you mean to go on. Purely by tone of voice, encourage good habits by unstinted praise and petting whenever deserved, and discourage the bad ones by a tone of disapproval. The first word a pup gets to know is usually his own name, but for heaven's sake don't be forever calling him by name or it will become quite meaningless to him. Call him when you definitely want him to come to you, rewarding him immediately and praising him when he does so. He must next be taught what "No" means, and when you say "No" to him it is imperative that you mean what you say.

Bringing a new puppy into the house, one of the first good habits to inculcate is that of house-cleanliness. But before attempting any of this early training, do grasp two facts – one being that no puppy can be expected to go all through the night without relieving himself; the other, that there are two specific times when he must do so, (*a*) on waking from sleep and (*b*) immediately after food. A puppy will seldom foul his own bed if he can get elsewhere, and if he has come from a good kennel he will have been accustomed from the moment he could first walk, to using some corner of the kennel floor just away from his bed, either on sawdust or a spread newspaper. Therefore prepare a corner in whatever room the pup is to sleep, by spreading newspaper, and be on the watch to place him there the very moment he wakes from sleep and immediately he has finished a meal. He very quickly gets the right idea. Each time he obliges and does as expected, praise him and tell him what a good dog he is. Associate the idea of "being a clean dog" in the appointed place by some simple word of suggestion, such as "get ready" or "make haste" or what you will, provided it is always the same phrase. This habit pays dividends in later life when you want the dog to hurry up and get his necessary jobs done. Thus cleanly habits in the house depend solely on the quick perceptions and commonsense of the owner. If you catch him "sinning" in the wrong place, never be rough with him but by tone of voice express your disapproval, at the same time picking him up and placing him where he ought to have gone.

A doormat or any sort of carpet offers a strong temptation to a pup, so instead of blaming him for using such instead of his own "lavatory", remove all mats before leaving him for the night.

Teaching a pup to go on collar and lead only requires a little time and patience if you set about it the right way. The essential thing is to associate happiness with the lead at the beginning. Use an old lead of no value for early lessons and let him play with it, chew it if he likes, while you play with him and put over the idea that it is all fun. He is getting to like it and that is what you want. When you eventually attach it to his neck, for only two minutes at a time at first, he will think this is all part of the game. Make these early lessons in leading very brief and always happy. If you or the pup become irritated, give it up till another day. Have a titbit handy when he is attached to the lead, and reward him every time he comes along and responds to your guidance. The whole process is to associate enjoyment in the dog's mind with the appearance of a collar and lead, so that ever after he reckons it a privilege to be "all dressed up" and taken to new sights, sounds and smells of interest. Never use the harness form of control; it encourages the dog to pull hard on the lead and at the same time ruins his front. And never by any chance use his lead for punishment. This immediately undoes all the early impressions that the lead is a happy thing. Also never leave a collar on a young puppy. This can have dire results, especially if he is not the only one but has some canine playfellows. A near-throttling has occurred from one puppy getting its teeth stuck into another pup's collar; besides which, a single pup can get into sundry difficulties by his collar catching in projections of various kinds.

Developing the habit of obedience comes into ordinary everyday life, if the owner is ever on the alert to encourage and praise by tone of voice each time the puppy responds and does what is wanted. Never shout at, or lose your temper with him, and never hit him. Of all breeds, this kind of treatment has a most disastrous effect on a Scot, making him shy, sullen, distrustful of strangers and, worst of all, losing his confidence in his owner. If he disobeys, he must only be checked and reproved when absolutely in the act of doing whatever it may be, and then only by your disappointed and disapproving tone of voice. The Scot has an innate desire to please, if we have the patience to realize this, and is terrifically sensitive to tones of voice and human emotions. Only in this way can we inculcate in him a sense of right and wrong.

EXERCISE. Scotties are extremely adaptable so far as exercise is concerned. Tough enough to enjoy a ten mile walk if accustomed to it daily, they can also keep perfectly fit with only a ten minute outing on a lead, plus a few brisk runs around a garden. That a walk on a lead, however short, preferably on a hard road for the benefit of his feet, is desirable every day if possible, is proved by the delighted antics of a well-brought-up dog at the sight of his lead being got ready. It contributes to his happiness, and happy dogs are the only healthy ones. Many Scots enjoy a game with a ball and can derive much beneficial exercise from having it thrown for them, but do be warned against the danger of leaving a ball with him, to be chewed up. Deaths caused by dogs swallowing bits of rubber (and there has never yet been a ball manufactured which is utterly indestructible) are far too frequent, and this should never be risked. A house dog will get quite a lot of exercise by merely being around house and garden all day, but if a dog is kennelled for some portion of each day his exercise must be regular and systematic.

Remember that a loose dog anywhere, except on his owner's property, is a public menace. If a person has no yard or garden in which the dog can be loose, then he or she had far better not keep a dog at all. All exercising in public places should be done on a lead. It is no hardship to the dog provided he gets enough of it and can indulge in some freedom at home.

If he accidentally gets wet during his exercising, be very sure he is thoroughly dried on returning home. A brisk rub all over, with particular attention to legs and underbody, with a chamois leather kept for the purpose, is useful for indoor dogs. A dog housed in an outside building can be rubbed dry very quickly in a deep box full of dry sawdust, while taking care none of its gets into his eyes.

CLEANLINESS. This heading applies not only to the dog's house manners, but to the abode he occupies, especially the bed he sleeps in, and to his own person. Keep his home as spotless as your own. His bed should be thoroughly brushed out once a week, to free it of all the hairs and grit that accumulate, and whatever bedding is used must be shaken out daily and replaced with clean as often as necessary. A good form of mattress for the sleeping box can be made by filling a sack cut to fit with crumpled up newspaper or wood shavings. The contents can be burnt at intervals and the casing washed. If blankets are used, wash them every week at least, using a good soap without detergent, and be sure they are bone dry before being used again. If at any time a disinfectant has to be used, avoid any containing carbolic, and in any case use very sparingly for if the dog is kept properly clean by daily grooming there should be no need of it.

The cleaning of the dog himself comes about by careful grooming. If combed and brushed all over every day he should never need a bath. Washing in any case ruins the coat texture and renders the dog liable to chills. A swim in a pool or the sea if the dog is keen about it, is a different matter, for the cold water does not penetrate his dense undercoat and a shake and a brisk run afterwards soon dry him off. But this should be only a warm weather pastime. Make the grooming session the occasion for a complete overhaul of all details, such as eyes, ears, mouth, feet, and under the tail. If you suspect all is not well with eyes or ears, consult your veterinary surgeon at once. Pay careful daily attention to the mouth while the pup is getting his permanent teeth at about five months old, in case any of the old milk teeth are preventing the new teeth from coming through properly. If this is noticed, have the offending milk teeth removed. Very often they are loose enough to press out with thumb and finger. Most puppies cast their milk teeth without much trouble, but the process is made easier for them if at this stage there is always a beef bone handy for gnawing, and if crisp rusks form one of the meals.

If a dog gets regular exercise on hard roads it is unlikely his claws will get too long, but if they have a tendency to do so use a carpenter's coarse file to rub down the tip of each claw to a comfortable length. Watch especially that the dewclaws on the inner side of each front leg do not grow long, for these can cause much discomfort to the dog by growing round in a circle into the flesh.

The coat, by reason of daily grooming, should be kept at all times absolutely free of tangled or matted hair. It is important to accustom a puppy to daily combing and brushing all over, so that in later life he does not resent such handling. One meets sometimes with Scots kept as pets, which have been allowed to get the upper hand and will not tolerate either the owner or anyone else combing out tangles under the hind legs or behind the tail. Strict attention should always be paid to keeping this area clean; with scissors keep the part immediately around the anus clipped short, so that no excreta can become stuck to the hairs causing the dog considerable discomfort and rendering him most unpopular with his human acquaintances. It is never the dog's own fault if he smells unpleasant.

Even a well kept dog may at times collect a flea from one of his less fortunate brethren or from other animals, so a weekly dusting of "Pulvex" into the coat, especially through the summer months, is a wise precaution against fleas, lice, or other unwanted vermin. Take great care that none of this powder gets into the dog's eyes.

7

BREEDING

DOG BREEDING, to a true dog lover, is an absorbing and interesting occupation. It can also be both pleasurable and profitable, or it may prove a headache and a total loss, according to the luck of the game. But luck is mainly good management. It requires patience, optimism, perseverance, tireless energy and at all times the strictest attention to details, and is a full-time job. For this reason it should not be undertaken unless there is a partner or helper available on whom the owner can rely to be left in charge occasionally.

Before embarking on breeding, be sure suitable facilities exist for the housing and care of the in-whelp bitch and for raising puppies. Letting a bitch have a litter for the benefit of her health, or rearing a few mediocre puppies to bring in a little pocket money is not serious dog breeding. The true breeder aims a lot higher than that. He looks ahead; he has a set scheme to pursue; he weighs up possible results not only from a first mating but from subsequent generations. He retains always the best bitch puppy from each litter, until, with a certain amount of luck, a lot of perseverance and the increased knowledge in selection which comes from experience, he has built up a strain of his own and bred specimens more nearly approaching the ideal. And in the doing of it he will have contributed something worth while to the breed in general.

The beginner is advised to start, if possible, with an adult bitch that is a proved breeder, and a young bitch puppy which can be growing on in readiness for being bred from later when the first bitch is taking a rest. Do not keep a male dog at first. Even if he should suit on type and pedigree both your bitches. it is waste of money to feed a dog year in year out for mating only a couple of bitches. There is a wide selection of dogs advertised at public stud, at fees ranging from three to ten guineas.

An inexpensive way of making a start in a breed is to take a bitch on breeding terms, but there are very seldom good ones to be had, since proved brood bitches which are easy whelpers are the "geese that lay the golden eggs", and not likely to be loaned by any sensible breeder. However, if terms of this sort are ever arranged, both parties to the contract should have a signed agreement, preferably one registered with the Kennel Club, from whence forms for the purpose can be obtained. A typical example of such terms is when the lender pays the stud fee or lends the bitch already mated, and from the resulting litter has first and third pick of the puppies, after which the bitch becomes the property of the borrower.

A bitch comes in season for the first time somewhere between seven and ten months of age. A swelling of the vulva is followed by a coloured discharge, which may last from ten to twelve days, or longer. Thereafter she comes in season every six months. It is unwise to mate a bitch at her first heat. Scotties have not done growing till about eighteen months to two years. The second or third heat is best for mating for the first litter. The best moment for mating is when the coloured discharge has only just ceased, leaving the bitch still swollen and a little damp. If taking the bitch to the stud dog, it is therefore essential to hit upon the right day when she is at her most willing. Stud dog owners however, often prefer to have the bitch before she has quite finished colouring, and keep her a few days so that the right moment to obtain a good mating is found.

In selecting a stud dog to suit your bitch, aim for one which resembles the bitch in general type and outline as far as possible, yet with improvements. Blending sharply contrasting types is never successful. Do not imagine that because your bitch has large soft ears, or maybe is weak at the pasterns, and you put her to a dog excelling in these particular points, that the pups will all take after the sire. Some may and some won't, but you have no guarantee that even the few which do will reproduce their sire's virtues in the next generation. Aim rather for a *gradual* correction of any faults the bitch may possess. For example if the bitch is a shade long-backed do not choose an ultra short-backed dog for her, but one which is of just moderate proportionate length. Some of the progeny will have moderate length of back, showing a slight improvement on the dam, and these again should be bred to dogs of medium and balanced body-length, not to exaggerated shortness. In this way gradual improvement on each generation bred is far more sure.

The factor, however, most to be depended on for effecting a gradual improvement in one's stock is in-breeding, if judiciously used. And this does *not* mean that the practice of in-breeding will of itself bring success. It will not create good dogs from inferior stock, except perhaps by careful selection over a very long period of years. What it does is to intensify and fix the points which are already in the stock in-bred to; therefore it is obvious such stock as is used for the purpose must be good, since in-breeding stamps any inherent bad features just as surely as good features. For instance one may mate a bitch to her sire, or a dog to his grand-dam, or full brother and sister, or any similar close combination, but if either parent possesses even the slightest tendency to shyness this will be increased two-fold in the resulting puppies, so that we may have a litter of beautiful idiots of no use to anybody; nothing is gained and much lost. Mental soundness, stamina and virility are more important than all else; make no mistake about that. Line-breeding is similar to in-breeding, but is a longer way round to reach the same destination, yet is less risky. In-breeding means mating very closely related individuals, but line-breeding is the practice of introducing the same blood, but not necessarily through the same individuals. For the novice breeder it is safer to advise a certain amount of consanguinity of blood when choosing a sire, provided the blood to be repeated is that of the best specimens in the two pedigrees, and to leave in-breeding to the more experienced.

The selection of a suitable stud dog is no easy matter, but certain principles should be observed. As remarked earlier, aim for a dog as similar in type to the bitch as possible – i.e. similar in carriage, conformation and size. Study the pedigrees of any prospective dogs together with that of your bitch, noting if there is any link-up of blood among the better known names in the two pedigrees. Try, by dint of enquiry, to gain some knowledge of the outstanding characteristics of the immediate ancestors. If possible, see the dog you think of using, in his own home surroundings. Temperament is not always revealed accurately in a show-ring and is of enormous importance in a sire. Just as in the selection of the bitch for breeding, pay special attention to the female blood behind the sire. Most dogs transmit the qualities of their own dam rather than those of their own sire, therefore avoid using a stud dog whose bitch blood is unimportant and does not trace to one of the recorded Families. Assuming that pedigree, type and temperament all appear suitable, then aim for the truly masculine looking dog which has plenty of bone and substance and a strong personality. The light-boned small dogs can occasionally be of use to a breeder with a certain set scheme in mind, but in the main they do not make the best sires. Above all do not be misled into thinking that because a dog is the latest sensation on the bench, or is a Champion, he must necessarily suit your bitch. A dog becomes a Champion solely on external merit, but until his hidden ability to get stock as good as or better than himself has been proved, he may be worthless as a sire. It is a fact that many of the breed's most impressive sires have not been Champions.

Once having decided which stud dog to use, care must be taken to ensure that the bitch is in the very pink of condition long before she is due in season. She must be free of worms and clean and healthy as to skin, and must on no account be fat. A bitch to be bred from should have lots of regular exercise, and be in hard muscular condition, rather on the lean than the fat side, since this renders it easier for her during pregnancy and when whelping.

Find out if the dog you have decided to use is likely to be available about the time your bitch should be in season, and book a service to him plenty of time ahead. In the early part of the year some of the popular sires get very much booked up. In case the one you want is too busy have a second choice in mind. Pay the stud fee at the time of mating. This is payable irrespective of whether the bitch proves in whelp or not, but in most cases a free mating is given at her next heat should she miss. This, however, must not be taken for granted.

Back home again after mating, the bitch should be kept fairly quiet for a few days, and definitely until she is over her heat. Some bitches remain in a mateable condition for several days. Cases have been known where the bitch has mated again twelve days after the first mating. When she is back to normal she can resume her usual routine as regards feeding and exercise, except that she must not be subjected to any jolts and jars, nor be allowed to chase a ball. The more her diet consists of good lean meat the better, with correct additions of cod liver or halibut oil, and calcium powder, but be careful not to overfeed her at first.

The period of gestation is sixty-three days, though Scots generally whelp a day or two early. Some, however, go over their full time, but so long as the bitch is behaving normally and not running a temperature, this need not cause anxiety for a couple of days. By the fifth week it is usually apparent if she is in whelp, and it is safer to assume that she is even if her abdomen is not noticeably larger. If she is carrying only one or two pups, some bitches are clever at disguising their pregnancy until the last week.

From her fifth week increase her food very gradually. Do not add to the bulk of the evening feed but make the addition take the form of a small mid-day feed of lean meat or a raw egg. For the last week cut out all starchy foods entirely, and instead of her morning rusk or biscuit get her accustomed to a milky drink for her breakfast.

It is desirable to be in touch with your veterinary surgeon when a whelping is in prospect. Let him know the expected date well in advance, so that if you do happen to need him at short notice he is more or less prepared.

For the last two or three weeks at least, the bitch should feed and sleep in the place in which she is expected to whelp so as to feel thoroughly at home in it. Nothing is more calculated to destroy her peace of mind than to be moved at the last moment. The main requirements about a whelping-place are that it must be warm and quiet, well away from all possible disturbances and especially out of sight or sound of other dogs. The box should be quite big enough for the bitch to stretch herself at full length, the floor of it being smooth with no cracks or crevices in the wood. The warmest form of box is covered in, with only the front left open for the bitch to get in and out over a low ledge. The top should be hinged to form a well-fitting lid, to make inspection of mother or pups easier. Recently the immense value of an infra-red lamp, especially in the winter months, has been proved by dog breeders, and if one of these is used and suspended above the box, the latter must of course have no lid, or else the lid can be hinged back out of the way when the lamp is switched on. Such lamps can be strongly recommended but must be used with discretion and hung quite three feet above the floor level of the box in which the puppies are. As the puppies grow on, the lamp should be raised further from them bit by bit until it can be dispensed with altogether.

Whatever bedding is provided will all be scratched out and torn up by the bitch when she begins to whelp, so a few layers of newspaper meets the case. Paper is warm to the body while the bitch spends some of her time sleeping, and when it is soiled is easily burnt and a fresh layer supplied for the new-born puppies.

The temperature of the whelping chamber should never be less than sixty-five degrees. Keep a thermometer hanging either in or close by the box and check up frequently, for human impressions of heat and cold are seldom reliable. Even in the middle of summer it is seldom warm enough at night for pups to be born without the provision of some artificial heating, and bitches invariably choose to whelp at night or in the small cold hours of the morning. So be sure that all arrangements for maintaining the whelping place at an even temperature night and day, are made well in advance. More young puppies are lost from being chilled at the start than from any other cause. Winter born pups cost more to rear and are infinitely more trouble than summer ones, but if artificial heat can be provided right on till they are twelve weeks old at not less than sixty degrees, and dry spacious play space available for them,

December to February is an excellent time for a litter to be born, for the better weather and the sunshine so essential for them come along just when they are of an age to benefit most.

Nearing the date for whelping a strict watch must be kept on the bitch, lest she indulge her natural instinct for going to ground or digging herself into a burrow or some other inaccessible place, as many of them do at such times. About three days before she is due to whelp, add a tablespoonful of liquid paraffin to her supper.

When she starts to tear at and dig up her bed in real earnest you will know the whelping is fairly imminent. This sort of preparation may go on at intervals for twenty-four hours or more before she actually begins to labour. Keep careful watch on her at this time, as unobtrusively as possible, to know exactly when she starts to strain really vigorously. She will pant a good deal, breathe quickly, and show every sign of restlessness, and will probably also vomit, but all this is the natural preliminary to a normal whelping. One person only should wait upon a whelping bitch, preferably of course the owner or whoever it is to whom the bitch is most accustomed, and in whom she trusts. Let her get on with her instinctive preparations undisturbed, merely taking a quiet look every half-hour or so. From the time of the onset of true labour pains, it may be a matter of two or three hours before the first puppy arrives. But if this has not happened within four hours, call in your veterinary surgeon without further delay. The whole litter may be lost, and possibly the bitch as well, if she is left too long in labour without skilled attention. Quite often the first puppy is an over-big one, and once this is safely delivered by means of expert assistance all may be well and the rest may be born easily.

In a normal whelping without any complications, the bitch manages everything for herself. As she expels each puppy she rips off the containing envelope, severs the cord by which the pup is attached to the afterbirth, and consumes the afterbirth. She then has a very busy few moments, alternately cleaning herself up and licking the puppy vigorously to dry it off. The pup itself, if alive, will have its mouth open to take gasps of air into its lungs, and most likely soon emits its first cry. It is natural then for the bitch to rest herself, and she will curl round the puppy to keep it warm until the next one is due to come along. Anything from half an hour to two hours may elapse between the births. Some bitches get very restless again before each birth, and some like to come out of their box and move around a bit. This is perfectly natural and should not be interfered with, but it is also one of the moments when the owner can be really helpful. The puppy or puppies left in the box while the mother wishes to stretch her legs will be still a bit damp, none too warm and proportionately miserable till mother comes back and can settle down again. So a hot water bottle wrapped in flannel should be ready at hand, on which to lay these damp firstborns and keep them warm, also help to dry them by hand by rubbing and rolling them about in imitation of the mother's tongue. This must be done in their box. The bitch does not like to see one lifted out at this early stage, but she will soon realize that the human aid towards warming and drying is really all in her own interests, and she will not thus be distressed by the cries of her pups while concentrating on her labour to get the next one along properly. When all the pups are born, the bitch usually settles down around them for a good rest, and soon after that it should be observed whether they are all suckling. In a healthy vigorous litter, so long as they are crawling and climbing in the general direction of their mother they soon will find their way to the teats, but if any seem specially slow about it or are getting crowded out, it can help matters to push them up against a teat and squeeze a little of the milk into their mouths.

When the family is all thus cosily settled down, check up to make sure the temperature of the whelping place is up to sixty-five degrees, and remove the hot water bottle for which there should be no more need. Then leave them undisturbed, and do not imagine the mother wants food for she is far better without. The wise provision of Nature that the dam consumes the afterbirths, ensures that she has all the nourishment she needs for the first day or two. The only refreshment safe or wise to offer her after whelping is a small drink of warm milk and water and honey. After the first twenty-four hours and for the next three days, she must be fed only on sloppy and fairly relaxing foods, such as gruel and milk, groats and milk, Bengers, etc., all being duly sweetened with either glucose, sugar, or honey, and given slightly warm. It is essential to keep her bowels fairly loose at first, solely by correct feeding, and no meat whatever should be allowed during these first three days. If all is going well by that time, her normal diet can be resumed, and from then on feed her well, three times a day while she is suckling the pups, using good lean meat, the occasional egg, and once a day the feed should be a milky one. If a bitch is thus fed properly while nursing a litter and the pups taught to lap at three-and-a-half weeks old, she should finish up in as good condition after the litter as she was before. By the time they are five weeks old she will have little further use for them apart from playing with them .

At a week old and from then on every few days, it is essential to snip the sharp points off the front claws of every puppy, with a pair of sharp scissors. If this is not done, their scratching claws while suckling can make the dam's udder so sore and tender that she may either tire of her task too soon, or may turn on one of the pups and damage it.

As soon as the pups are of an age to take notice and toddle around, never give the dam her food in the place with them. Also keep her away awhile after her meals, lest she vomit up her food for the puppies' benefit as many bitches will do. When, after five weeks old, the pups are provided with the big beef bone to gnaw, be sure and remove this before letting the dam go in with them.

VIII. WALSING WAR PARADE. Black brindle dog bred by Mr. W. M. Singleton, about 1944.

X. REANDA ROSITA. lack brindle bitch red by Mrs. E. Meyer, 949. Famous as the am of six Champions.

X. CHAMPION BIDFIELD BIX. Wheaten dog bred by the Misses Payne & Harrold. Born 1950.

XI. A litter of wheaten puppies and dam bred by Mrs. P. Leonard in 1954.

XII. JASCOT JACQUELINE. Wheaten bitch bred by Mrs. N. Peake. Born 1956.

8

PUPPY-REARING

PUPPY FEEDING starts as early as three-and-a-half weeks, while still with the dam. At first this consists only of learning how to lap from a flat saucer. As soon as they have grasped the idea, reduced milk is the best thing to give them for the first few days. This is arrived at by allowing a pan of fresh milk to stand on a slow heat for about half a day until it has reduced and thickened to almost half its original bulk. Goat's milk is better than cow's if it can be got. Naturally, at this tender age the amount of such supplementary food the pups will consume is infinitesimal, but, even so it helps to relieve the strain on the dam's own milk supply, especially if she has four or more to rear. For the first few days they will not need this additional feeding more than once or twice day, but by four-and-a-half weeks old their meal-times should be regular at four-hourly intervals four times a day. Gradually accustom them to other forms of nourishing baby-foods, such as Bengers food, Groats, Ostermilk, or similar preparations, and now and then a raw egg beaten up in warm milk. Every milky feed given them must be sweetened, either with glucose, honey, or sugar. At this stage, one must watch out that the dam does not have a chance to vomit her own food for the pups. It is an instinct among the best mothers to do this, just as in a wild state the bitch vomits her pre-digested food for the litter until such time as they are old enough to go out into the world and battle for themselves. But under our civilized conditions there is danger in it, for the dam's half-digested food may consist of substances quite unsuitable for the youngsters, and may be lumpy and cause choking. So keep the dam away from her pups for a couple of hours after her meals when the pups are around this age.

By five weeks old, one of the four meals per day should be scraped raw beef. Lay a thin slice of best lean meat on a board and with the edge of a knife scrape all the pulp away from th fibrous part. Feed the pulp only, at first only a teaspoonful to each puppy, increasing it gradually as time goes on. Naturally this feed must be given separately to each puppy. For their milky dishes, a litter of pups can all feed from the same dish together, taking care the stronger among them do not have it all their own way and so crowd out the smaller or weaker ones. But from six weeks onwards, most of the meals are better given separately, otherwise there is no way of knowing if some are getting too much. Most owners who love their dogs will have identified each puppy with a name of its own by this age, and feeding time offers an excellent opportunity for the puppy to realize its own identity. Call one by name, place it on a table or bench to eat its tiny portion of food, holding it steady the while by tail or hindquarters. Repeat the routine with each puppy. This way they learn very quickly that it pays to come when called. It is waste of time and good food to put down anything meaty and appetising among a bunch of pups, only resulting in squabbling and possible choking.

By seven weeks, cooked meat, either boiled or roasted, can be used for one of their meals. Always use the best lean, mince it very finely, and avoid giving any gristle. Gristle can cause fits in young puppes. Whatever food is given, never offer more than will be cleaned up readily and quickly. Much more harm is done by overfeeding than underfeeding. In a week or so the condition of a puppy will soon prove if you are erring in either direction. Overfeeding will make him look blown out after a meal and causes diarrhoea. If he looks consistently pot-bellied in between meals, it is one of the signs that he needs treating for worms. Underfeeding will soon cause him to lose weight and will encourage in him a depraved appetite for all the wrong things such as coal, shoe-laces, stones, bits of wood—in fact everything that a pup will chew but should NOT be allowed to eat.

"Little, often and good" is the maxim for successful puppy feeding, and regularity of meal-times is most important. So, too, is variety of food. Never give the same food at two meals in succession. As a guide to correct feeding of a Scot puppy from eight weeks to four months, ring the changes on the following suggestions:—

7.30 or 8 a.m.

A. Tea-cupful of warmed milk thickened with Farex or wheat-flakes and sweetened with either honey, sugar, or glucose.

B. Raw egg beaten up in warm milk with a teaspoonful of thick honey.

C. Small quantity of well-cooked porridge, with milk and honey or sugar added.

D. Robinson's groats, Bengers food, or Ostermilk wel sweetened.

12 noon

A. Scraped or very finely minced raw beef.

B. Shredded wheat or similar cereal moistened and softened with good unseasoned gravy or broth.

C. Cooked lean meat, very finely minced, on which sprinkle a few rusk crumbs.

D. Stale wholemeal breadcrumbs moistened with good unseasoned gravy.

4 p.m.

Every day at this time a drink of warm milk and honey.

8 p.m.

Supper, selected from one of the 12 noon suggestions.

Note: To one of the meals each day add 2 drops of cod liver or halibut oil per puppy and to another add Dene's 'Nature-bone' (calcium powder) according to age as given in directions on the tin. By gradual degrees, accustom puppies to the addition also of finely chopped parsley, grated raw carrot, or chopped raw cabbage to some of their meals. Do not give cooked vegetables, and never potatoes. Supply a large raw beef bone from time to time, giving it to them after a meal, never before. A section of shin-bone is best. Get the butcher to saw through a shin bone into four pieces, and not smash it, but be sure to remove any loose bits of broken bone or gristle before letting the pups have it. They will derive plenty of entertainment working the marrow out for themselves.

Alternative food-stuffs suitable for growing puppies and

which aid variety are well-boiled tripe (the uncleaned sheep's paunch is best for them), or sheep's head, or breast of mutton. In the case of either of the latter, the very greatest care must be taken, having first boiled it to rags, to allow plenty of time for picking over and removing all bones. Though a dog's digestion can deal with raw bone; any sort of cooked bones are most dangerous to him and should never be allowed.

By the age of four months, three meals a day are sufficient. Make the mid-day feed a bit later by degrees and ultimately cut out the 4 o'clock milk. Gradually accustom the puppy to drier food. Rusked wholemeal bread is a great standby. Put slices of stale brown bread into a slow or a cooling oven at every opportunity, and store the resulting crisp rusks in an airtight tin. Once or twice a week, the mid-day lunch can consist of nothing but a few of such rusks. Especially is this helpful around the teething stage of four to five months, and at any age a crisp rusk is as good as a toothbrush to the dog. After eight months, the feeding can gradually take on the routine suited to an adult dog.

All puppies have round-worms, so all puppies should be treated for them at eight weeks old without fail, and before being passed on to other owners. The best remedy is "Ruby" (obtainable from all chemists) if the directions are followed implicitly. If the pups show signs of worminess earlier, by perpetual pot-bellies or by vomiting, this remedy can be safely used at six weeks. Until that age, if worms are suspected, make more generous use of raw eggs in the diet, as this will tide things over till they can be dosed.

Puppies need an immense amount of sleep. Their bouts of play can be frequent but should be short, and when they fall asleep afterwards make sure they do so in a cosy and sheltered place and not on cold or damp surfaces. Pups ought never to get even their legs and feet wet, but if it ever happens, dry them off quickly.

9

EXHIBITING AND SHOW PREPARATION

THERE IS immense satisfaction to be derived from proving that one's own stock is worth while by pitting it against others in competition and gaining some awards. To be successful as a breeder does not necessarily entail exhibiting, but without doubt a few prize cards won in good company add greatly to the prestige of the kennel and render the sale of its surplus stock the more likely. To the serious breeder showing is an absolute necessity. Dog shows provide the only test available to us of the merits and consequent value of our stock, and are one of the best forms of advertising. Present-day costs make dog-showing an expensive pursuit, and in itself it cannot be said to be a paying one, except indirectly as a means of publicity, for the dog show is in a sense the breeder's shop window. It is also an occasion when much can be learnt about dogs in general and your own breed in particular.

Beginners are advised to make a start at a small Open or Members' show and ignore the Championship events until they have gained a little experience both for themselves and for their exhibits. Avoid the mistake made by so many, of selecting Crufts great show for your first appearance in a ring. Forthcoming dog shows are advertised in the weekly papers *Our Dogs* and *Dog World*. One applies for a schedule and then discovers whether there are any classes listed for Scottish Terriers. Every dog has to be registered at the Kennel Club with a name of its own before it can be shown, and if you have bought the dog the transfer of ownership has similarly to be registered before exhibiting the dog in your name, so make sure all is in order in this respect before making any entries.

Many months before the date of a show at which you intend to enter your dog, you must begin to concentrate on his condition, his coat, his trimming and his ring demeanour. All these factors play a very big part in the possible success of your exhibit, quite apart from his individual merits. Many opportunities of winning prizes have been lost by unusually good terriers being presented in the show-ring either right out of condition or completely untrained for the job.

We will assume you had the dog stripped at the correct time—i.e. when the outercoat is dead and loose—and that you have him in nice form as regards flesh, not carrying too much fat, nor yet thin, but in firm muscular condition, and in the buoyant responsive state of mind resulting from such good condition. The daily grooming keeps the coat clean and helps it to grow along evenly, and the dates of any shows in prospect must be chosen to best suit the rate of coat growth of the dog concerned.

Scots cast their coats every six months on an average. As soon as the outercoat shows signs of being dead and loose, the process of casting it is usually speeded up by stripping. This is mainly for the purpose of attaining an even effect all over, for if left to itself the dead coat certainly comes off eventually, but rather piecemeal fashion so that the dog looks untidy the while. Many owners ruin their dog's coats by too frequent and too forcible stripping before the coat is really ready to be done. It is wiser to assist Nature and work with her than to go against her methods by dragging off a coat that is not by any means dead.

Correct stripping consists of removing by finger and thumb all the dead outercoat from *all over* the dog, except his head and throat. These areas are dealt with by clippers, since hand stripping or removal with a trimming knife can be too painful for the subject. The "all over" includes the legs and the underbody, where what are called the furnishings grow to excess. If these are not taken off, at any rate at the first total strip, which usually takes place at about nine months old, they will never look well with subsequent coats. The rate of coat growth varies a bit with individuals, but one can reckon most Scots are not going to be in good new coat for show until three to four months after stripping.

About six weeks or less after stripping is the time to start, concentrating in all seriousness on keeping the prospective exhibit shaped out by trimming. Just as with grooming, it has to be a daily concern. Do not expect to achieve a finished result at one session; it is a case of a hair here or a hair there; as the new coat grows fast on some parts and slower on others, you have to make use of this fact by letting it develop where it is most wanted and keeping it in check by shortening or thinning where it is liable to get too profuse. All the time you must have an ideal in your mind to work to, and shape your dog accordingly as far as possible. There is real artistry in skilful trimming, and the best presented dogs are usually those on whom a little time is spent every day for months prior to a show.

The tools you will require are (a) stripping knife, with serrated edge, (b) ordinary barber's scissors, (c) a pair of thinning scissors, and (d) clippers. Some owners prefer to have two sizes of clippers, one small and fine for taking the hair down close on the backs of the ears, but these are not really necessary, since the normal sized clippers will do the job, and the edges of ears are best done very carefully with scissors.

Do the trimming of your dog on a sturdy bench or table that is of sufficient height from floor level to work at without bending your back. This gives you a better view of the dog, and if you fix a mirror behind the bench so much the better for judging effects as you proceed.

It is not really possible to learn how to trim a Scottie to advantage from a written description, though one may pick up a few useful hints. Far the best way to learn is to get a few practical demonstrations from an experienced exhibitor, when you are fortunate enough to find one in the right mood with time to spare.

Starting with the head, on the top surface of the skull from ears to eyebrows the hair must be kept short. Work in a forward direction with the clippers, that is against the growth of the hair, but on no account start too near the ears, or carry on too far forward to spoil the eyebrows. A small amount of longer hair is left in front of the ears, and to form becoming eyebrows, and these parts are kept tidy with scissors. Keep studying the effect as you go along, remembering that you can never put back any hairs you have taken off, so work slowly at first. Leaving a little hair in front of the ears makes the ears look smaller, which is usually a help to most specimens, but any surplus hair at the backs of the ears should be taken off, as well as every suggestion of a fringe at the edges of the ears. Keep brushing the eyebrows and the hair on the foreface forwards as you work, and you may find it improves expression to trim out a little from between the eyes, when dealing with the eyebrows. Too much heavy eyebrow or too much "fuzz" on the top surface of the muzzle detracts both from the expression and from the apparent length of head; and again, with eyebrows, do not leave spikes or tufts of hair projecting sideways beyond the outer corners of the eyes.

Now in imagination picture a loop of string drawn round the dog's face the upper part of the loop being just on or slightly behind his eyebrows, and the lower portion of the loop passing under the muzzle, roughly half way between chin and throat and consequently further forward than the top part of the loop. All the hair in front of this imaginary line is to be brushed in a forward direction and, within reason, can be left as profuse and dense as the dog cares to grow it. But do not cultivate a beard like a goat's nor let the whole thing become tangled. Take due note while brushing whether a profuse beard suits the style of head, or whether judicious trimming with scissors makes a more tidy effect. Any of this scissoring should not be done within the last fortnight of a show, otherwise the ends of the hair will show they have been cut. Half the art of trimming is to give the impression that the coat grows the way you have it and that no trimming has been done.

The hair on cheeks and front of throat, behind this imaginary line of string, has to be kept short with clippers. Do not work the clippers, however, too far down the chest, nor too far back at the sides of the face where the hair tends to form a ridge below each ear-base. These areas must be kept tidied with a stripping knife, merged carefully into the longer coat on back and sides of neck, down the lower part of the chest, and grading off at the sides of the shoulders so that there is no line of demarcation noticeable between the shorter (clipped) hair and the longer body coat. The back and sides of the neck and down over the shoulders will need probably more work, both with thinning scissors and stripping knife, preparatory to a show, than any other part, for it is here the coat grows most quickly. Keep combing the dog as you trim and aim for an even effect. The line of back from withers to root of tail should look as level as possible, so study the dog's outline in profile and trim a little at a time wherever necessary to attain this effect. Tails ought to be of moderate length, thick at the root and tapering to a point, so even if the dog is not blessed with a perfect tail much can be done when trimming to create the impression of a shapely and proportionate appendage. Leave the coat to grow pretty thick at the root end of the tail, reducing the growth gradually and evenly to about half way up its length; from there to the tip shape it off to a point with the scissors.

Trimming the rear end to get the best effect is not easy but comes with practice and knowing the construction of the dog concerned. Immediately under the tail this area should at all times be kept closely trimmed with scissors but for show you have got to arrange that from the root of the tail, over the hips and down towards the hocks, the hair is nicely blended into the furnishings which will be left in moderation on the hind legs. View the subject from all angles while working, and frequently put him down on the floor to have a shake and a run around while you take due notice of just where you need to trim more. Viewing the hindquarters from the rear, the effect of being moderately wide and very muscular must be retained, but do not allow a bunchy effect on the hips, nor too much suggestion of voluminous baggy trousers lower down. According to whether the dog is broad built or narrow, shorten or encourage the growth of coat down the thighs. Viewed from the side, a gentle curve over the "seat", merging smoothly downwards to the hocks, should be aimed at, with no untidy spikes of hair projecting to spoil the outline, and never leave profuse bunches of hair above and around the hocks as is far too often done. It merely detracts from the overall outline of the dog and arouses suspicions that all is not well with the anatomical construction of the quarters.

Front legs have got to be made to look thick, straight and

sturdy, so one has to trim them with that end in view. Usually it pays to reduce the hair a bit on the *outer* side of each foreleg from the elbow joint to a point half way down the leg; and on the *inner* side of each leg where the slight bend of pastern occurs. These portions are best done with a stripping knife, and all the time be careful to keep combing the hair and blending in to an even effect.

Then all four feet have to be looked to. Having combed each leg, hold the dog with his weight on the foot you are trimming, and with the scissors remove any excess fringes or spikes of hair so that you form a nice looking firm round foot. Toe-nails must of course be examined daily, and kept short by filing. Nothing spoils a foot or the movement of a dog, more than overlong nails.

Last, but by no means least, all the trimming in the world, and all the physical attributes your dog may possess will count for nought unless he has been well schooled in ring demeanour. If he has been a well brought up puppy he will have learnt to love his collar and lead, but should he not have been so fortunate, this is the first essential. The show dog must associate being put on a lead with everything that spells enjoyment. Once attain that, the battle is partly won, and you next task is to get him doing exactly what you want when on the lead, and at the time you want it. A little daily lesson, however short, is desirable. Most exhibitors use a very narrow but strong collar, and a lightweight but equally strong lead, but some prefer a slip-cord. There are many varieties of such things, but, whatever you select, use the same thing every time for the preliminary training and on the day of the show, for the dog gets used to it. In any case avoid using a ponderous collar an inch wide, or a chain instead of leather lead. The outfit should be as unobtrusive as possible, since it is only the dog that is being judged. Each lesson should consist of a routine such as this; attach collar and lead and with the dog led on your left side, have some tasty titbits in your right hand. Lead him to some space – maybe a room, or a yard, or a lawn – and pretend it is a show-ring. Teach him first to walk up and down in a straight line with you. Then to walk nicely on your

Top Winning Dog Ch. Gaywyn Lively Lad : owner Mrs Owen

Colour photos by Anne Cumbers

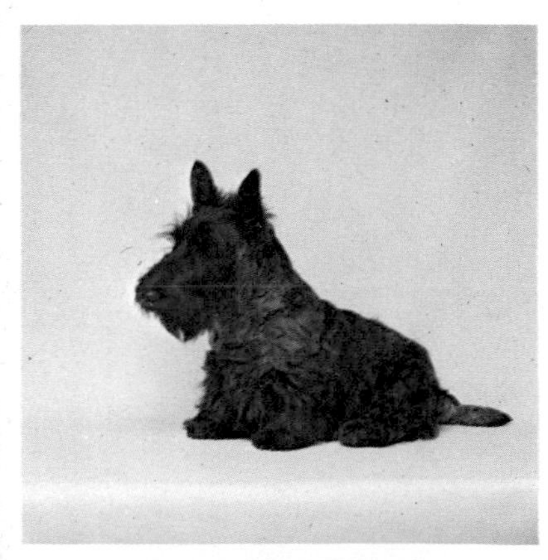

Gaywyn Clock Watcher

Mayson Christie : owned by
Mr and Mrs Gaskell

Mayson Christie being
groomed

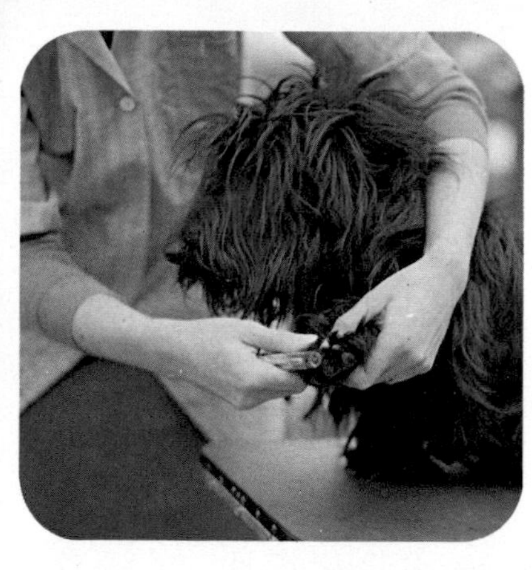

Nails being cut

Neck only being clipped

Gaywyn puppies being handled by children at an early age

Gaywyn puppy: owner Mrs Owen

left in a circle to the left, as is done in a ring. Always, when he has moved nicely and responsively with tail and ears alert, neither pulling on the lead nor dragging backwards or sideways, reward him with a titbit. Then you teach him to stand smartly, solely by reward at the right times. He should learn all this by your movements and the guidance he receives from the lead, but there is no harm in talking to him as well, encouraging him and praising when deserved, though only the quietest tones are needed since his hearing is much more acute than yours, and too much chatter is out of place when you finally get into a ring.

Do not make any lesson in show-ring deportment last longer than a few minutes at a time, and never long enough to get you or the dog feeling bored with it. If possible, get a few other people to stand around while giving the show-lesson, to prove that neither yourself nor the dog need take any notice of them. The object in view is for you and the dog both to be concentrating on the dog showing well, so that other distractions make no difference. Next lift the dog on to a table, as he will be so treated when he gets to a show, and accustom him to being handled all over, teeth, feet and all else, without protest. Let as many people as possible also handle him, so that he accepts it all calmly from friends and strangers alike.

When all this routine has been well and truly learnt at home, then you must put his show demeanour into practise in other places. Try him near a busy road, where passing pedestrians or traffic may quite likely take his mind off the job. Take him pub-crawling and have him so well trained to respond, that at the word of command from you and for the accustomed titbit when he deserves it, he will display his showing ability in the centre of the bar to the admiration of your fellow-drinkers. Until you have attained a confident, devil-may-care attitude on the part of the dog under all sorts of circumstances, so that he completely ignores all distractions and shows himself off smartly when required, don't imagine you have one ready to take to a show. It is not fair to the dog itself, or to you, or to the person who has to judge it, to take an untrained and inexperienced exhibit into a show-ring. Naturally some individual dogs are what is called "born showers" and are then much easier to educate than others, but even these require a little training to respond correctly at the right time, and in the wrong hands even good natural showers can make at times a very indifferent impression in the ring, if the handler is not concentrating on their looking their best all the time.

And when finally in the ring, this is the main secret of success in ring craft – concentration on the business in hand to the exclusion of all else. The business being to display your dog's virtues to the best advantage, *never* for a single moment while in a ring take your eye off your dog. One eye on the dog and the other on the judge is the best rule. Don't waste your energies keeping the dog at his alert stance while waiting for other exhibits to be examined, but have him ready promptly at the crucial moment when the judge looks your way. Good ringcraft may be summed up by three C's: Concentration; Confidence – you need enough of this to impart some to the dog – and Calmness. A lot of unexpected things may happen to you in a ring, including being sent out without a prize, but don't let anything worry you.

10

THE STUD DOG

IF IT is intended to use a dog for stud purposes he should be allowed to mate his first bitch at about nine months old, and it is essential that this bitch should be specially selected for his benefit. She should be middle-aged or elderly for preference, one that has mated easily and bred several times before, and one known to be of a docile disposition and easy to mate. Some young dogs are very slow to get the idea of what they are expected to do, and if left too long, maybe to only fifteen months or so, without ever serving a bitch, are apt to be silly about it and waste a lot of time merely tiring themselves out and provoking the bitch unnecessarily.

Provided the dog gets a successful mating with his first "practise" bitch, do not use him again till he is over twelve months old, and then only twice at most between that age and eighteen months. Scottish Terriers are not fully matured until eighteen months, and many take till two years to come to their best form. Too much stud work when young will check a dog's development and the litters he sires are likely to lack virility. Also he may tire of the whole business—for all the bitches he mates will not be easy ones—and then be no further use at stud. After he is two years old, and from the age of three and onwards, if he is kept in the vigorous hard condition befitting a stud dog, he may, if a popular and successful sire, mate as many as a hundred bitches in a year. In the busy season, from about February to May he can serve as many as three a week for a short spell, but if worked to this extent he should be allowed quite a month's rest after the rush.

Before introducing a bitch to the dog be sure she is in the best stage of her season for mating. Also that she is clean, healthy in skin and not overfat. Usually bitches are at their most willing stage from the twelfth to fourteenth day of their heat. Right from the start, let the dog understand that every bitch he is expected to mate will be held steady for him throughout the mating. Even though his first practise bitch is utterly placid and co-operative, hold her just the same. In this way the dog soon realizes there is no sense in rushing madly around chasing his lady friend and making many false attempts to mate her, till both are hot and breathless, when by waiting for the bitch to be firmly held in a suitable position his job can be made fifty per cent easier for him, and his sexual urge satisfied all the sooner. It is the custom with small breeds to place the two to be mated on a platform or table, so that the dog's owner is saved the back-breaking business of holding the bitch steady on the floor. A long bench or table up against a wall is safest, for no risks must be taken of either animal jumping or falling off during the performance.

The most satisfactory procedure is first to let the two view each other through the kennel railings or a wire fence. If the bitch is really ready the fact should be apparent from her coy behaviour. She may growl at the dog one moment and strike inviting attitudes the next, but by and large this will mean she is taking an interest in him and doesn't want to lose sight of him. Then, in one of her more amiable moments, let the two run together in an enclosed space well away from interruptions, and if the indications are favourable they will warm up with a sort of preliminary flirtation until the bitch decides to stand invitingly with her tail curled to one side. At this stage, and quickly before the dog has time to fool about and waste his energies, pick the bitch up on to the table, and hold her firmly by the collar while you grab the dog, who by that time, if he is a keen stud, will be so eager to follow her that his springing ability towards the table-top coincides with your lifting hand. Then, holding the bitch's collar or scruff of her neck firmly with one hand, use the other hand for both keeping her tail out of the way and slightly raising her vulva to make penetration more easy for the dog. Do not handle the dog in any way, until, when a tie is effected, and he turns round off the bitch until they assume a back-to-back position, you can ease him round gently. Then continue to hold the bitch quite still and quiet until they separate in the normal course of events. A tie is not absolutely essential, for once the dog has penetrated the bitch he may be steadied in the mounted position for merely a few moments, when a litter should result just as well as if there had been a tie. The tie, if one occurs, may last anything from five to fifty minutes, or longer.

Should the bitch show signs of snapping at the dog when they first meet, even though she encouraged him through the fence, take no chances of his getting badly bitten, and cut out the preliminary flirtation altogether.

The items one should put ready on the mating table in advance are a small fibre mat for the dog to work from as this gives his hind feet a better grip; a selection of short bits of board of varying thicknesses for slipping under the mat in case it is found the bitch is a bit tall for the dog; and a jar of vaseline. It eases matters always to insert a well-vaselined finger into the bitch before mating, and by using the whole length of one's finger it provides opportunity of knowing if she is roomy and easily mateable, or small-made and tight. Mating with the latter sort will usually only be effected by the most vigorous and determined of stud dogs.

Never let your dog serve a bitch until quite four or five hours have elapsed since his last meal. Also be sure that both dog and bitch before mating have had ample opportunity to empty their bowels and bladder. This is most important. After mating, put both away quietly in their separate kennels far away from each other, with fresh drinking water, and let them rest for an hour or more.

If visiting bitches are going to be accepted to your dog, special accommodation must be arranged for housing them. They may be brought over for mating on the right day, or they may be sent several days in advance from a distance and possibly be in your care for about a week or longer. In either case there must be comfortable, safe and hygienic housing for them, right away out of sight and sound of other dogs, where artificial heating can be provided in cold weather, since a large number of bitches used for breeding are also house-pets.

In selecting a potential stud dog, there are certain points to keep in mind. His pedigree should bear the closest scrutiny, preferably show some line-breeding to his best ancestors, and be particularly good on the dam's side. He must not only be good in himself but should excel in temperament, having a proud bearing, confident demeanour and a look of masculinity. Usually the best sires have one or other of the desirable features slightly exaggerated; it may be head, or weight of bone, or general solidity and great depth of rib.

It does not necessarily follow that because a dog is good and possesses all the external virtues plus the right disposition, that he will make an impressive sire. The "proof of the pudding etc.", and only from the stock he sires from a variety of bitches can we judge whether his influence is valuable or otherwise. Occasionally quite faulty dogs prove exceptionally good sires, but it is found the blood behind them is of the best and it so happens that they possess the capacity to transmit the good features of their antecedents without passing on their own failings.

The belief that a dog if used at stud cannot also be a satisfactory pal and house-dog is ridiculous and has no foundation in fact. A well brought up intelligent dog can be equally efficient in both capacities; the only difference is that, whereas your house-pet may rough it occasionally as regards food, or make do with fairly uninteresting meals on some nights in the week, the dog used for stud work must have the very best feeding all the time. He needs to be fed like a hard worker, which he is if used at all often. A generous use of raw eggs must be added to his diet, and by dint of regular exercise, daily grooming, together with all that contributes to a dog's health and happiness, he must be kept in hard muscular condition at all times. Particularly is this important if he is to be placed at public stud. The discerning breeders like to see a dog in his own home surroundings before deciding to use him, and since they may drop in at any time of year it pays to keep the stud dog not only fit to be seen as regards skin and coat but in absolutely tip-top condition for twelve months out of the twelve.

Owners of a nice-looking well-bred dog are often under a delusion that someone will be glad to mate their bitch to such dog, either for a stud fee or for a puppy in lieu of fee. They find it difficult to understand that others are not as mad keen as they are themselves to have some of this dog's progeny. But before a dog can demand any outside patronage, let alone a stud fee, he must have some definite qualifications. Usually he has to prove his individual merits on the show bench first. If he has not been good enough or had the chance to do this, he must have sired a few outstanding specimens which have gained notoriety by doing some winning. Practically every owner of a breeding bitch will prefer to use a dog that has sired winners to one that has not. And the choice of stud dogs available in our breed to-day is wide indeed. There is no justification for using an unknown unshown dog when there are so many to choose from. Moreover in nine cases out of ten, such a dog would not know how to mate a bitch.

The stud fee is always payable at the time of mating, and is due for the services of the dog irrespective of whether puppies result. If any other arrangement is made, such as the owner of the dog taking a puppy instead of fee, this should be set down in writing and signed by both parties. Should such a plan be agreed to, state which sex and at what age the puppy is to be handed over, and if only one puppy should result the owner of the dog is entitled to it without question.

New owners of a stud dog which has aroused enough interest to get used are often in some doubt as to what fee to charge for his services. While still a youngster under two years and with a few minor wins to his credit, it is reasonable to start him off at three guineas. By the time he has won his own way into the K.C. Stud Book and proved he can sire worthwhile puppies, he can be raised to four guineas. As a sire of winners he can demand five guineas, and this to-day is a very average fee for dogs which are not Champions. Champion dogs can demand anything from six to fifteen guineas according to their owner's evaluation or to the frequency with which they are being used.

The above subject, together with all else pertaining to the breed, is dealt with more fully in my book *The Popular Scottish Terrier*, published 1956.

11

TRAVEL

MOST SCOTTIES are good travellers, and when accompanying their owners in whatever form of conveyance it may be, usually love the experience. Their innate adaptability and chamois-like sense of balance fits them for all sorts of modes of travel. One has known individual dogs cover considerable mileage in side-cars, on pedal cycles, in bath-chairs, perambulators and boats of all types. Whatever Master or Mistress chooses to get around in, the Scot pal prefers to share it rather than be left at home. As for motoring, it is rare to encounter one of our breed that does not genuinely enjoy it. It is also rare to find one affected by car-sickness, but if there is any tendency in this direction our veterinary surgeons can now supply small pills for the canine travellers which overcome it.

Motor cycling is not to be recommended if the side-car is an open one, for the dog is far too exposed to wind and weather which will sooner or later cause trouble with both eyes and ears. It is not always realized, however, that similar troubles can arise in a closed car, if precautions are not taken to ensure that the dog is not riding in a perpetual draught. Probably the majority of drivers and front seat passengers in a car have never sampled a journey in the back seat, yet they cheerfully allow the dog to occupy the back seat without discovering first just how much draught may be blowing on him when the car is travelling at speed. If your car is that sort, and cold air from ventilators and windows blows around the interior towards the rear the comfort of any travelling Scot can be assured by providing him with a covered box. The front end of it should be open, or have a wired door, so that he still has the pleasure of seeing where he is going, but the solid top to the box excludes all down draughts which can play such havoc with his ears. Most Scots prefer this arrangement and will choose to jump into such box, knowing it is cosy and their very own. It is not only desirable in cold and wet weather, but almost equally so in the occasional hot weather, for then people drive with all the car windows open and it does the dog passenger no good to be blown to smithereens all the journey, He will be cooler and safer in his box.

Hot weather motoring offers several problems for dogs since unless the greatest care and watchfulness is exercised they can suffer the tortures of the damned. While it is seldom in this country that a dog dies from intense cold, excessive heat can and does kill, when the dog is in an enclosed space from which he cannot escape. Whether from heart-failure or heat-stroke, for a dog to pass out thus in a car is a cruel and ghastly death solely due to its owner's negligence. When motoring in hot weather, never go without a bottle of water and drinking bowl for the dog. But the main trouble is the stationary car. The thoughtless owner parks the car with a dog in it, in the sun. Though it may mean but a five minute call, it is long enough on a hot day to cause the dog infinite distress. It has to be remembered that the coachwork and glass of the modern car attract the sun's rays just like a greenhouse, and the amount of heat generated inside, even with all windows open an inch or two, can be quite unbearable. When shopping and leaving a dog in the car, the obvious remedy in hot weather is never to park except in the shade of houses or trees. And here again common sense is needed, for if leaving the car for any length of time the sun will be shining from quite another direction when you return to it, and you must take this into consideration.

Never let your dog passenger travel in a car with his head poking out of a window. This is simply asking for eye and ear trouble.

Your dog may have to travel by rail. There are two ways he can do it. Either in a safe travelling box, in which case he goes in the luggage van, or on a lead accompanying his owner. Small dogs such as Scots are usually allowed in the carriages, where, if well behaved, they are generally popular; but if you are unlucky enough to meet up with a fellow passenger who is anti-dog, be prepared to remove yourself and dog to another carriage. Make very sure before starting on a journey this way that the dog's collar is sound and fitting him closely, and that his lead is strong and safe. The noise and bustle of a railway station is no place for risking a slipped collar or a broken lead. If sending a dog by rail unaccompanied be very particular about his box. It should be strong yet light-weight, as the rates for dogs in boxes are charged by weight. There are good aluminium and also three-ply boxes on the market. Make sure the size of the box suits the dog; he should have ample room to stand up and turn round in it, but not too much waste space so that when being lifted and moved he pitches from end to end of it. The ventilation of the box should be plentiful, on all four sides and in the roof of it as well. The dog itself generates a lot of heat in a closed space, and while the ventilating holes must not be so large as to allow his nose to push through, do remember that he needs all the air he can get, and that there have been far too many cases of dogs found dead in unsuitable travelling crates due to suffocation.

The subject of travel includes the possibility of one taking a dog or two on holiday. With this end in view, it is a wise precaution to accustom every dog from its youth up to being chained up for short periods. While in his normal home surroundings there is probably never any need to tie him temporarily to a table-leg or to the chair you are sitting on, but when staying at an hotel or in the house of a friend you (and incidentally your friends) will be mighty glad your dog has learnt this accomplishment in advance so that he will remain tied up without protest whenever required.

If holidaying abroad or anywhere your dog cannot go, it may be necessary to make use of a boarding kennel for him. Care should be taken to select a kennel where the accommodation and care given to the inhabitants appears satisfactory. Call and see the place beforehand, and observe if possible whether the other boarders look happy. It is just as essential to book holiday accommodation for your dog well in advance as it is your own hotel. Some boarding establishments house a hundred dogs or more, but this is no reason to assume they can fit in an extra one at short notice. All boarding charges should be paid promptly on collecting your dog, or, if he is there for a long period, it is best to settle the account monthly. Every dog is accepted at such kennels at owner's risk, and it should be clearly understood that though every reasonable care is taken of him no responsibility is accepted for illness, accident, or death from any cause. Boarding fees for Scotties may be anything between fiftteen and thirty shillings per dog per week; artificial heating provided in cold weather, special medicinal diet, treatment, or any damage your dog may do to his kennel while there, are all extras to be charged for quite legitimately.

A dog can be taken to and brought back from Ireland or the Channel Isles without undergoing quarantine on re-entering this country, but from all other countries he has to spend six months in a quarantine kennel.

If taking or sending a dog by air, there are a number of regulations to be complied with and documents to be provided. It is necessary either to contact one of the Air Lines in advance to obtain full details of all the formalities, or you can employ one of the Shipping Agents who will undertake to arrange everything on your behalf. For most countries an Export Pedigree, issued by the Kennel Club, is needed, as also is a Veterinary Certificate of health in duplicate. When an air journey is anticipated for any dog, do be sure to give that dog preliminary practise at being shut in a travelling box for a few hours each day for several days before he has to travel. Tough enough to have to experience all the noise and movement, without in addition having to grow accustomed to the confinement of a box.

12

KEEPING RECORDS

HANDY KENNEL-RECORD books can be purchased, or the owner can make one up at home, in which every detail such as date of birth, breeder, and pedigree of each dog owned; prizes won, with date and place of show and name of judge; stud visitors; litters of puppies raised – can all be recorded. It is most desirable to put these facts on record rather than trust to memory which is seldom infallible. Such a record book provides interesting reference in the years to come, especially if additional details regarding the progress of puppies are entered, such as the weight of each puppy at certain ages. In the copying and entering up of pedigrees, the very greatest care should be exercised to ensure accuracy of every name, particularly the spelling. In some pedigrees one finds that repeated small mistakes made by first one and then another can result in the names of quite famous antecedents becoming unrecognizable.

Further items of which it is desirable to keep records are details of all sales made and the price received, or of purchases and the price paid. Also of breeding terms if such are undertaken. The amount of secretarial work arising in a well-ordered kennel of any size is considerable. Copies should be kept of all advertisements published, so that subsequent reference can prove which style of advertisement brought the best results.

13

COMMON AILMENTS

SO SUSCEPTIBLE to suggestion is the ordinary mortal who owns a dog, that you have only to remark on the wonderful results from using Vetzyme, Benbow's Mixture, or Bob Martin's powders – or whatever it may be – to send them running to buy the same thing for their own dog. And whether in need of it or not the dog is given a course of one patent medicine or another. If a dog is kept, fed, groomed, exercised and trained on the lines indicated in the foregoing chapters he should, barring accidents, seldom require any corrective medicines.

However, for the simple disorders which may crop up at home, here follow a few hints.

The first thing to impress upon the average owner is that on the first sign of indisposition on the part of the dog, keep him in, where a comfortable temperature prevails (between fifty and sixty degrees) and keep him quiet, and give him ABSOLUTELY NOTHING to eat, until such time as you may by observation diagnose what the trouble may be. Small quantities of slightly warmed drinking water, in which you have placed a small teaspoonful of honey, may be offered at intervals, but do not leave water with him for the time being. Watch him carefully, take his temperature, check his pulse, and give Nature a chance by fasting him.

The dog's temperature is taken by inserting a slightly greased clinical thermometer into the rectum very gently and holding it in place for a minute while the dog is kept quiet and steady. If the thermometer does not slide in easily, do not exert pressure but change the direction of it either upwards or downwards and try again; it should be inserted to about half its length.

A dog's normal temperature is about 101 degrees. If you find it 102 or even another half degree up, there is not a lot to worry about, unless two hours later you find it still higher.

But 103 or more degrees strikes a warning note of possible danger ahead.

The pulse is checked by placing a finger on the artery to be found on the inside of the thigh. A little practise will soon get you used to finding the right spot. The number of beats per minute should be roughly about ninety.

Most of the simple disorders affecting the average pet dog are of gastric origin, usually due to mismanagement and generally to incorrect feeding. Many people labour under the delusion that the Scottie is prone to eczema, but this is a complete fallacy. He is no more susceptible to it than any other breed, and if and when he becomes so affected, again it is due to a faulty diet.

If all dog owners would study and practise Homoeopathy, it would be a great deal better for the dogs. The remedies advised in the following list of possible disorders are mainly homoeopathic, and where this is the case a capital "H" appears in brackets after the name of the remedy. All homoeopathic remedies and advice on the treatment of dogs, can be obtained from Epps, Thatcher & Co., of 60 Jermyn Street, London, W.1.

ABSCESS. An abscess may develop on any part of the dog, usually due to injury, such as a bite, and is indicated by swelling of the part with inflammation and a rise of temperature. Treated with promptitude the condition can be quickly relieved. Bathe the affected part with Calendula (H) lotion and administer pills of Belladonna (H) and Hepar Sulph (H) alternately.

ANAL GLANDS. This is not an ailment, but when a dog is seen to be rubbing itself along the ground in a sitting position, it is often mistakenly suspected of having worms. In nine cases out of ten this behaviour merely means that his anal glands require attention. Since the domesticated dog is not usually fed on a sufficiently constipating diet, the action of his bowels does not clear these glands of their secretion as it would in a state of Nature. Consequently this should be done by hand about every third week, to maintain a dog in perfect health, otherwise anal abscesses may form. Apply the tips of all four fingers and the thumb firmly and closely around the anus, while grasping the dog's tail with the other hand, and then exert a combined squeezing and pushing movement, which, when done properly, will press out all the unwanted secretion. It will squirt out in all directions and smells objectionable, so be warned in advance.

BILIOUSNESS. Due to too rich or unsuitable food, the dog vomits bile and lacks appetite except for water, but appears to be in no pain. Podophyllum (H) is the remedy, three times a day. Curtail the drinking water somewhat and do not feed.

BLADDER. Keeping a dog too long without a chance to empty its bladder is a most frequent cause of Cystisis, or Inflammation of the Bladder. It can also be caused by chill, or exposure to damp. The dog strains ineffectively to pass water, is very blown-out, the abdomen being painful when touched, there may be some fever and his pulse is quickened and taken all round he looks pretty miserable. Prompt relief can be given by pilules of Aconitum (H) every ten minutes at first, followed by Cantharis (H) every two hours. Give barley water for a day or so; no other food.

BOWELS. Exposure to intense cold or wet, or subjected to sudden changes of temperature, may result in inflammation of the bowels. Fever is present, the dog shivers and may cry out with sudden sharp pain, is unduly thirsty, and may have diarrhoea. Withhold all food, allow only a spot of water, and treat with Belladonna (H) and Colocynth (H) alternately.

BURNS OR SCALDS. Boric acid ointment should be applied, covered with cottonwool and bandaged into position. Change the dressing twice daily. If none of this ointment is available, a quick alternative treatment is to spread flour freely over the burn and bandage it until the ointment can be got.

CATARRH. Indicated by coughing and sneezing, with a

watery discharge from the nose and, if no fever present, is quickly cured by keeping the dog under observation for a day or two while giving him Arsenicum iod (H) every three hours. Similar symptoms may occur at the start of Distemper, so the temperature must be taken immediately at the first sign of a cough or cold.

DIARRHOEA. Can be caused by too much food, the wrong sort of food, a chill, or by feeding from a dirty dish. If an adult, keep without food except for a little arrowroot with milk, or well-boiled rice in milk. No meaty foods at all. The best cure is two tablets of Mercurius Cor: (H) every two hours, for a day. If young puppies, give China officinalis (H) tablets instead, and withhold all meat, feeding lightly as above.

DISTEMPER. Immunization against both Distemper and Hard-pad is much practised nowadays by inoculation. If a dog contracts it after he has been inoculated, he is likely to have only a mild attack which responds quickly to good nursing. In fact, whether inoculated or not, good nursing, similar to that given to a human with influenza is the main secret of successful recovery. Diagnosis is important since there are so many possible symptoms. Early signs are listlessness, lack of appetite, possibly vomiting and diarrhoea, and usually a watery discharge from eyes or nose or both, a husky cough and a definite rise in temperature with an accelerated pulse. Immediate isolation is necessary if Distemper is suspected. It is very contagious. The dog should be kept quiet in an even temperature and never let out of the room he is in until cured. Homoeopathically, when aided by competent nursing, a cure is normally assured. Alternate dosing with Aconitum (H) and Arsenicum Alb: (H) every two hours night and day, is the treatment. The sole nourishment offered to the invalid should be nothing but warm water with a little honey in it. And as he improves a little milk can be added, but be very chary of letting him resume normal life afterwards until the temperature has been normal for three or four days.

EAR CANKER. If this is persistent it is best to consult the

veterinary surgon, as there are an infinite number of different kinds of ear canker. If only slight, however, a little Borocal Powder (H) dusted into the ear, together with dosing on Mercurius Sol (H) will effect a cure.

ECZEMA. May arise from general mismanagement, or the presence of worms, but mostly to wrong feeding and over-feeding. It is not contagious, and if the diet is corrected and internal treatment given by Arsenicum (H) tablets every four hours one day and Sulphur iod: (H) similarly the next day, continuing thus alternately for a fortnight, is usually easy enough to cure. External treatments do little good, but to overcome the soreness and irritation of any affected patches, dust on some Borocal Powder (H). Some individual Scots cannot digest a too generous ration of meat, so if a case of Eczema arises, try reducing the meat allowance and add more raw vegetables and fruit if he will take it, to the biscuit meal and rusked bread.

GASTRITIS. Is inflammation of the stomach, indicated by pain, a great thirst, and sometimes vomiting, plus a rise of temperature. Withhold all except an occasional spoonful of slightly warmed water, and give alternately Belladonna (H) and Mercurius Cor: (H) until the patient is relieved. The cause is all too often the swallowing of small (or cooked) bones, which the dog should never be allowed.

INDIGESTION. If a simple stomachic disturbance, shewn by vomiting, thirst to some extent, and flatulence, give Nux Vomica (H) tablets three times a day. Or, if accompanied by diarrhoea, give Carbo Veg (H). The latter is particularly curative and reviving to elderly dogs.

MANGE. This is of two kinds, Sarcoptic and Follicular. The first is highly contagious, the second not at all. If either are suspected, consult expert veterinary advice immediately.

RHEUMATISM. Indicated by extreme stiffness, most often

affecting the back and hind legs, and can be caused by lying on a cold surface too long, or from a damp bed, or by not being vigorously dried after a wetting. Cimicifuga (H) every two hours, is an unfailing remedy, giving Aconitum (H) last thing at night.

WORMS. For youngsters too old to dose with Ruby, give Chenopodium (H) tablets night and morning. For adults, use Filix Mas (H) tablets night and morning for four days, then a dose of Castor Oil. Most dogs are subjected to worm treatment far more often than they ever need it. First make sure his anal glands are in good order and properly squeezed out at regular intervals before dosing the dog for worms unnecessarily. Also, to remove the intestinal condition which is inclined to encourage the presence of worms, give a liberal dose of Liquid Medicinal Paraffin on the supper once a fortnight.

14

BREED CLUBS

THE FOLLOWING specialist Clubs exist for the purpose of encouraging the breeding of pure Scottish Terriers, to urge the adoption of the correct type on Breeders, Judges, Dog Show Committees, etc., and to advance the interests of the breed in every possible way. The name of each Club secretary in office at the time of writing, is given in brackets.

THE SCOTTISH TERRIER CLUB (ENGLAND). (Mrs. G. D. Yates, 42 Barnet Avenue, Bents Green, Sheffield, 11.

THE SCOTTISH TERRIER CLUB (SCOTLAND). (Mr. A. P. Allan, Marne, Johnstone, Renfrewshire).

THE NORTH OF ENGLAND SCOTTISH TERRIER CLUB. (Mr. M. G. Birchenough, 23 Wesley Road, Armley, Leeds, 12).

THE NORTHERN COUNTIES SCOTTISH TERRIER CLUB. (Mrs. M. E. Jackson, 49 Grange Road, Bury, Lancs.).

DURHAM AND NORTHUMBERLAND SCOTTISH TERRIER CLUB. (Mr. J. C. Bousfield, Triermayne, Nevilles Cross Bank, Durham).

SCOTTISH TERRIER BREEDERS AND EXHIBITORS ASSOCIATION. (Miss P. Drummond, 7 Fern Cottages, Little Marlow, Bucks.).

WEST OF ENGLAND SCOTTISH TERRIER CLUB. (Mrs. A. V. Richardson, Ashley Lodge, Box, Wilts.).

NORTH MIDLANDS SCOTTISH TERRIER CLUB. (Mrs. G. D. Yates, 42 Barnet Avenue, Bents Green, Sheffield, 11).

SOUTH WALES AND MONMOUTHSHIRE SCOTTISH TERRIER CLUB. (Mr. M. G. Scanlan, 40 Newfoundland Road, Gabalfa, Cardiff).

ULSTER SCOTTISH TERRIER CLUB. (Mr. A. Gordon, 306 Albertbridge Road, Belfast).

BIBLIOGRAPHY

ASH, E. C. "The Scottish Terrier". (London, 1936).

BUCKLEY, H. "The Scottish Terrier". (London, 1913).

CASPERSZ, D. S. "Scottish Terrier Pedigrees" (Henley-on-Thames, 1930).
"The Scottish Terrier". (*Our Dogs*, 1938).
"Scottish Terrier Pedigrees". (Henley-on-Thames, 1934).
"The Scottish Terrier Handbook" (Nicholson & Watson, London, 1951).
"Scottish Terrier Pedigree Supplement" (Henley-on-Thames, 1951).
"The Popular Scottish Terrier". (Popular Dogs Publishing Co., 1956).

DAVIES, C. J. "The Scottish Terrier". (London, 1906).

EWING, F. C. "The Book of the Scottish Terrier". (New York, 1932. Revised ed. 1936).

GABRIEL, D. G. "The Scottish Terrier". (London, 1928. Second ed. 1934).

HAYNES, W. "Scottish and Irish Terriers". (New York, 1912).

JOHNS, R. "Our Friend the Scottish Terrier". (London, 1932).

KIPLING, R. "The Supplication of the Black Aberdeen". (London, 1931).

MAXTEE, J. "Scotch and Irish Terriers". (London, 1909).

MCCANDLISH, W. L. "The Scottish Terrier". (*Our Dogs*, 1909).

INDEX